STATEMENT CONCERNING PUBLICATIONS OF RUSSELL SAGE FOUNDATION

Russell Sage Foundation was established in 1907 by Mrs. Russell Sage "for the improvement of social and living conditions in the United States of America." While the general responsibility for management of the Foundation is vested in the Board of Trustees, the responsibility for facts, conclusions, and interpretations in its publications rests with the authors and not upon the Foundation, its Trustees, or its staff. Publication under the imprint of the Foundation does not imply agreement by the organization with all opinions or interpretations expressed. It does imply that care has been taken that the work on which a manuscript is based has been thoroughly done.

VOLUME 1 OF A SERIES ON THE SOCIAL CONSEQUENCES OF ABILITY TESTING

The SEARCH for ABILITY

STANDARDIZED TESTING IN SOCIAL PERSPECTIVE

by

DAVID A. GOSLIN

Associate Sociologist

Russell Sage Foundation

RUSSELL SAGE FOUNDATION

New York 1963

Printed in the United States
of America

Library of Congress
Catalog Card Number: 63-12591

WM F. FELL CO., PRINTERS
PHILADELPHIA, PA.

Foreword

THIS BOOK is the first in a series of reports on the social consequences of ability testing, for which publication is planned by Russell Sage Foundation. Dr. Goslin's study analyzes the striking change which has taken place in our society during the past half-century in the development and use of ability tests in assigning individuals to positions in society, and in creating opportunities for social mobility.

The increasing use of tests in the United States constitutes a change in emphasis from traditional bases for the determination of status, such as race, sex, religion, and order of birth, to a greater reliance on this new criterion, performance on a standardized test of ability. As Dr. Goslin points out, the source of this change can be traced to a number of factors, including the growing concern for education in America and the greater technological complexity of the society which makes it of increased importance that individuals occupy positions for which they are well suited. It is notable that the growth of standardized testing has come about as a direct result of the application of social science techniques to the solution of a problem; that is, how to select the best-qualified individuals for the various educational and occupational positions in society.

At present virtually nothing is known about what effects the testing movement is having on our society, and on the individuals who are directly affected by test results. The social consequences of standardized testing have not been considered systematically by testers or by social scientists, despite the expanding importance of the movement and the number of decisions being made on the basis of test results. In this vacuum of information about test consequences, an interesting body of folklore has sprung up; an example being the taboos against telling a child or even a child's family his score on an intelligence test. What, in fact, are the consequences for an individual of having knowledge about his abilities? This question, like the others posed throughout Dr. Goslin's book, has not been carefully investigated up to this time.

The central importance of ability testing in American society, the fact that its implications reach into many areas of modern life and strongly influence attitudes and procedures of the practicing professions, led Russell Sage Foundation in 1961 to undertake a program of research on the social consequences of testing. Because of the size and complexity of the research task, a series of interrelated and centrally coordinated studies is envisioned, to be carried out by the Foundation staff and by independent groups working with them. To assist in this task an Advisory Committee composed of leading behavioral scientists has been obtained. The members of this committee are Drs. Bernard Berelson, John H. Fischer, Wayne Holtzman, Horace Miner, Wilbert E. Moore, Talcott Parsons, Henry Riecken, and Ralph W. Tyler.

The first two studies in the program now have been started, with financial assistance from Carnegie Corporation of New York. The first of these concerns the beliefs and attitudes of the American public about ability tests and the way they are being used. In initiating a program of studies concerned with the impact of standardized testing on American society, the immediate prerequisite is information on the types of experiences which people have had with ability tests, on the kinds of attitudes which people hold toward objective measures of ability, and on the way people think tests are being used in this country. Providing an individual with information about his performance on an intelligence test, for example, is likely to have consequences for the person who believes that the scores represent his true ability that are quite different from those experienced by the person who has little faith in their accuracy. Similarly, if an individual believes the tests measure an unchangeable, innate set of aptitudes or abilities, test scores may have a more pronounced influence than where one feels the score represents a relatively changeable measure of achievement.

A related question concerns the way in which groups of people conceive of intellectual abilities. Traditionally, American values have emphasized the virtues and rewards of hard work and equal opportunity for each individual to achieve in direct proportion to his effort. On the other hand, the extensive use of standardized tests of ability in schools, business and industry, government, and the military places a greater emphasis on individual differences which are in part inherited and thus biologically based. The contrast between our own educational philosophy and the current point of view in Russia serves to underline the importance of the difference between these two conceptions of human abilities; one strongly influenced by genetic factors, the other viewing ability chiefly as the result of a rich and sympathetic environment. These differing beliefs about human ability, which characterize not only nations, but diverse groups within our own society, are likely to lead directly to differences in achievement motivation, creativity, and productivity of groups and of societies. Closely related as an issue are the views of the public with respect to the morality or the fairness of the use of ability tests in the process of allocating opportunities for advancement and reward in our society.

The second study now in progress will collect data about children's attitudes toward tests in school and their awareness of the existence of differences in abilities between children. In addition, the effects of school testing programs on a child's conceptions of his abilities, on a teacher's perceptions of and behavior toward students, and on parental estimates of children's abilities will be investigated. This will be done by studying schools making extensive use of standardized tests and disseminating information about the test results to school personnel, parents, and children, in comparison with other schools making little use of tests.

These two studies are the initial steps in a program of research on the social consequences of standardized testing. A number of additional studies are contemplated. One of these is an intensive analysis of the effects of testing on the individual's self-image, motivation, social adjustment, and on his actual opportunity for social mobility.

Another problem requiring research concerns the consequences of testing for the family. The potential impact of testing on the relations between siblings, between parents and children, and between spouses, should be evaluated systematically with a concern for changes in authority patterns, allocation of opportunities for different experiences and social advancement within the family, marital interaction, and related family processes.

Comparative institutional analyses of personnel selection and allocation procedures in business and industry, government, and the military should be undertaken in order to answer questions about the impact of alternative uses of tests on effective manpower utilization, employee morale, and organizational efficiency.

In providing the background for the projected research on the social consequences of testing, Dr. Goslin has chosen to look at the testing movement from a new perspective. His aim is to examine ability testing in terms of its social, legal, and emotional effects on the individual and the major institutions in society. His purpose is not to resolve issues, but rather to raise questions and at the same time to point the way to needed research on the consequences of standardized testing. He accomplishes these goals by reviewing the extent of ability testing and the variety of uses to which tests are put in our society today, and by setting forth an analysis of the many types of important effects which may follow from their use.

Although a primary purpose has been to provide a basis for the subsequent studies, this book will be of special interest to those who make use of tests, including school administrators, government personnel officers, and those involved in executive selection, and military recruitment and allocation. In addition to providing an overview of the major social movement in which they are key participants, it should help to draw their attention to some of the effects with which they should be concerned.

This book will also be of interest to behavioral scientists. While it is understood that psychometricians and others involved in test development will be familiar with a large part of the material presented by Dr. Goslin, many behavioral scientists will not. It is these who may gain a new perspective from this volume and perhaps will undertake studies of the consequences of standardized testing in society.

Orville G. Brim, Jr.

Acknowledgments

THIS VOLUME was made possible by the many persons and groups that contributed their knowledge, skills, and time at all stages of the project. Although the author is solely responsible for the accuracy of the opinions and conclusions expressed herein, it is clear that by far the greater part of what may be useful in these pages is the result of the contributions of many different people.

Perhaps more than to any other individual, the author is indebted to Orville G. Brim, Jr., for his encouragement, counsel, and constructive criticism from early discussions to the final editing of this volume. A careful reading of the manuscript by Henry Chauncey, president of Educational Testing Service, resulted in many helpful suggestions and thoughtful criticisms for which the author is particularly appreciative.

In addition, the author is grateful for the assistance rendered by the Advisory Committee and by the following persons in providing much of the factual material on which the conclusions are based: Miriam Aronow, Albert H. Aronson, John T. Dailey, Henry S. Dyer, Robert L. Ebel, Warren G. Findley, John C. Flanagan, Robert L. French, Edgar Fuller, A. O. Gamble, J. Thomas Hastings, John L. Holland, Francis A. Ianni, Martin R. Katz, Samuel Kavruck, E. Lowell Kelly, Roger T. Lennon, Kenneth F. McLaughlin, Albert Maslow, Ovid Parody, Alice Y. Scates, Harold G. Seashore, John M. Stalnaker, Lloyd Trump, Arthur E. Traxler, J. E. Uhlaner, Logan Wilson, and Dael L. Wolfle.

Finally, the author gratefully acknowledges the contribution made by Ann C. Goslin, who not only provided the encouragement necessary for the completion of the manuscript, but also added greatly to its comprehensibility, and Ryllis G. Lynip, who took on the difficult task of preliminary editing.

DAVID A. GOSLIN

Contents

Part Two

ABILITY TESTS AND PREDICTION

Part Three

THE NEED FOR RESEARCH ON THE SOCIAL CONSEQUENCES OF TESTING

Tables and Figures

TABLES

FIGURES

I

Introduction

ALTHOUGH INFORMATION about the extent of testing is sparse, it appears that between 150 million and a quarter of a billion standardized ability tests of many different kinds are being administered annually in the United States by schools, colleges, business and industrial firms, and government agencies, including the military services, in an effort to evaluate the intellectual capabilities of potential and existing personnel.

In spite of the extensive use of objective tests by many different groups, testing has become a source of controversy. Critics of current practices have become more vocal with the increase in test use. Test publishers and users, precariously riding the wave of acceptance, but feeling the undertow of skepticism, have gone to some lengths to reassure the tested public of the fairness of test instruments and the manner of their use. However, many people have refused to be convinced either of the validity of tests or the wisdom of basing selection procedures on test scores. As the public gains in its awareness of the extent and importance of testing in the allocation of individuals to positions within the society, it may be predicted that present differences of opinion with respect to testing will be sharpened. The ethics and effects of the use of tests are likely to become new battlegrounds in the dispute over testing.

The following chapters have been written in an effort to provide a basis for a program of research on the social consequences of testing. In addition to a survey of past and current practices in the measurement of intellectual abilities, an attempt has been made to clear up some of the confusion about testing and to suggest some of its possible effects on the society and its members.

Although by no means exhaustive of the theoretical consequences of testing, the last chapter indicates some of the problems awaiting systematic research in this area.

The material for the present volume was gathered from a variety of sources, including interviews with educators, test publishers, and psychometricians; reports of research on tests and testing; and statistics on test use published by schools, business firms, the government, and the military. Throughout the collection of data, it was the author's impression that all of those concerned with standardized testing, either from the standpoint of test publisher or test user, were very much committed to finding the answers to some of the questions raised on the following pages and to making the wisest use of our knowledge about the measurement of human abilities. The consensus of test publishers and users seemed to be that it was time a comprehensive program of research on the effects of testing was begun.

Ability testing, as the term is used throughout this volume, refers to the use of standardized tests for the measurement of intelligence, aptitude, or achievement. We have included in our definition tests that purport to measure abilities which for the most part reflect learning, as well as those designated as general intelligence and aptitude tests, because it is becoming increasingly difficult to decide where to draw the line between the innate and acquired components of measured abilities. It is clear that all tests must measure developed abilities, and many psychometricians have given up the terms "intelligence" and "IQ" with their connotation of innate ability, in favor of words such as "scholastic aptitude" that call attention to the contribution of the individual's environment as well as the purpose of the test.

Test standardization implies the establishment of specific and uniform conditions for administering the test, and uniform methods of interpreting the results. In addition to test questions that can be graded accurately by anyone regardless of his personal feelings or idiosyncrasies, standardization requires norms based on the test performances of a large number of individuals so that any particular score may be meaningfully interpreted. The most widely used technique for achieving objectivity in a written test is the multiple-choice question, in which the respondent is forced to choose one of several answers, thus eliminating subjective judgments on the part of the grader as to the correctness of the answer.[1] While "objective" tests can be criticized on other grounds,[2] most standardized ability tests, particularly those designed to be administered to a group of people simultaneously, are of this type. Throughout the remainder of this volume, the terms "standardized test" and "objective test" will be used synonymously.

Personality tests are not discussed in this volume, with a few minor exceptions. Primarily because of a lack of demonstrated validity, personality tests have not enjoyed the popularity that ability tests have received. Although personality tests are being used sporadically by industrial psychologists, it is the opinion of the author that thus far they have played a relatively minor role in personnel selection except in those cases where evidence of extreme deviance shows up in the examinee's performance.[3] Certain kinds of personality tests have been proved to be useful in the diagnosis and treatment of mental disorders, but for our purposes they appear to be of only peripheral interest at the present time.

This volume was not written in an effort to answer the critics of present testing practices or to provide fuel for new attacks on the testers. Instead, its purpose is to raise the issue of the possible social consequences of testing—both good and bad—and to suggest some of the ways in which we might go about investigating these effects. This goal has been sought within the context of a survey of the extent of ability testing in the United States. To the best of the author's knowledge, this is the first attempt systematically to describe testing practices in the various sectors of the society and, as such, it is intended to break ground for succeeding investigations. It is hoped that it will provide a useful as well as provocative perspective on a unique aspect of American life: the measurement of human intellectual abilities.

[1] Subjective judgments may be involved, however, in the selection of questions to be asked and in the designation of the correct answer.

[2] See, for example, Hoffman, Banesh, "The Tyranny of Multiple-Choice Tests," *Harper's Magazine*, vol. 222, March, 1961, pp. 37–41; and, by the same author, *The Tyranny of Testing*, Crowell-Collier Publishing Co., New York, 1962. Hoffman's criticisms will be discussed below.

[3] An opposing point of view, however, is presented by Martin L. Gross in his recent publication, *The Brainwatchers*, Random House, New York, 1962.

PART ONE
ABILITY TESTING IN AMERICAN SOCIETY

II

Ability Testing in Historical and Social Perspective

THE EVALUATION OF INDIVIDUAL ABILITIES is not a recent phenomenon. From the very beginnings of human society, men undoubtedly have compared themselves to other men with respect to their skill in hunting and fighting. Women probably have vied with one another in the preparation of food, the care of their children, and their ability to attract the male of the species as long as societally prescribed differences between the roles of men and women have made such comparisons appropriate. Children, no doubt, have been tested and graded ever since schools first came into existence, and before that, their abilities were carefully observed by parents, tribal elders, and above all, by their peers. In short, in the broadest sense of the term, testing has been going on for as long as human beings have been organized into societies and groups.

During the second half of the nineteenth century, however, several new developments radically changed the nature of this process of differential evaluation of human abilities. The first of these was a growing awareness that individual differences in intellectual abilities were potentially measurable in the same way that height and weight are measurable. The second was the development of probability statistics that made possible a conceptual yardstick against which a quality as difficult to grasp as human intelligence might be systematically compared. These two events, coupled with an existing value system in which ideas about individual differences in ability were encouraged to take root and a variety of social needs that focused attention on the forthcoming innovations, led to the invention of techniques for the testing of human intellectual abilities and set the stage for the spectacular increase in the use of these techniques which we have witnessed during the past fifty years.

From a sociological standpoint, the rapid development and increasing use of standardized tests of intellectual ability in the United States provides an excellent example of an innovation and its subsequent acceptance by the members of the society. In the past fifty years not only has testing become firmly established as a part of American culture, but the experience of taking a standardized, objective test of intelligence, aptitude, or achievement now is virtually universal among children and widespread within the adult population.

The fact that standardized testing is principally a western phenomenon, and in particular a characteristic of American culture, serves to emphasize that cultural values provide the context in which an innovation appears and is accepted or rejected by a society. High achievement and the opportunity for rapid individual advancement based on ability as well as initiative and hard work have traditionally formed the core of the set of values inherent in the "American way of life." While as has been pointed out by Myrdal and others,[1] the content of our value system has not always been translated into actual practice with respect to distributing opportunity for advancement equally throughout the society and ignoring such ascribed characteristics as race, sex, and family background, there has been great concern for finding better ways of distinguishing between individuals and rewarding unique individual ability. Abraham Lincoln, Albert Einstein, and Horatio Alger have provided our society with role-models that have focused attention on the rewards and accomplishments of high ability and hard work. In this setting it is not surprising that new methods for identifying individuals with unusual capacities independent of family background, sex, and race[2] found ready acceptance.

[1] Myrdal, Gunnar, *An American Dilemma.* Harper and Bros., New York, 1944.

[2] Acknowledgment should probably be made of the fact that, particularly in the early days of testing, standardized tests turned out to be a way of enforcing the disadvantaged position of some groups inasmuch as their relatively deprived educational status made it difficult for them to compete even on what were claimed to be tests of innate intelligence. While this is less true today, it is still a factor to be considered in evaluating the performance of minority groups on standardized tests.

In his analysis of status and role in human societies, Ralph Linton[1] pointed out that the better adjusted the members of any society are to their statuses and roles, the more smoothly the society is likely to function. Since the adequate performance of most adult roles requires considerable training, particularly in technologically advanced societies, Linton postulated that the earlier an individual's training for a position began, the more successful and complete it is likely to be, and consequently the more able the individual will be to perform his duties. If, however, the notion of differences in the desirability and difficulty of roles is introduced into this schema, we must face the dilemma of deciding which individuals to train for which jobs in the society, assuming that differential training techniques are appropriate and that competition for a limited number of high status positions is likely to make it necessary to choose from a large number of candidates. We have pointed out above that societies have typically used a variety of ascribed characteristics (for example, race, sex, and family background) in order to facilitate the making of early decisions about who will receive what kinds of training within the social system. The recognition that differences in innate ability do exist meant that some measure of these differences at an early age was potentially the most efficacious means (from a societal standpoint) of making such decisions; for example, choices as to who was to receive a college education. Since American values tended to lean in the direction of the development of "fairer" means of making these decisions about who was to have the opportunities to advance and hold high positions within the society, scientists began to look harder and harder for the means by which to measure differences in intellectual abilities in a more accurate and systematic way at an early age.

In the following paragraphs we will attempt to trace some of the major historical events[2] and some of the significant tech-

[1] Linton, Ralph, *The Study of Man.* D. Appleton-Century Co., New York, 1936.

[2] For a more detailed history of testing, see Goodenough, Florence L., *Mental Testing,* Rinehart and Co., New York, 1949; *Encyclopedia of Educational Research,* 1960 ed., chapter by Robert Ebel and Dora Damrin, entitled "Tests and Examinations"; Freeman, Frank N., *Mental Tests:* Their History, Principles and Applications, Houghton Mifflin Co., Boston, 1939; Boring, E. G., *A History of Experimental Psychology,* D. Appleton-Century Co., New York, 1929.

nological innovations which have had an impact on the growth of testing in the United States. These changes occurred within a favorable climate of social values, but a compatible cultural context is only one aspect of the process of culture change. An adequately developed technology is necessary for the introduction of an innovation, as well as the presence of social needs which focus attention on the emerging cultural product and ensure its acceptance. Our first concern will be with the ideological and technological innovations which immediately preceded the appearance of large numbers of standardized tests. Then we will turn to a consideration of the existing social needs which served to focus public attention on the new techniques and thereby contributed to the rate at which testing has become an integral part of our culture.

THE EARLY DISCOVERIES: GENETICS AND STATISTICS

In 1838 Esquirol wrote a three-volume treatise on mental disorder[1] which, for the first time, systematically attempted to distinguish between disease and mental deficiency. Although he did not make explicit the notion of inherited differences between individuals in this work, Esquirol did note that "idiocy is not a disease, but a condition in which the intellectual faculties are never manifested, or have never been developed sufficiently to enable the idiot to acquire such amount of knowledge as persons of his own age reared in similar circumstances are capable of receiving."[2] In addition, he went on to point out that different grades of mental deficiency exist in different individuals and that a method for distinguishing the feebleminded from the normal was needed.

While increasing numbers of medical people and a lesser number of educators were becoming interested in the problem of feeblemindedness, both in the United States and abroad, Charles Darwin was laying the groundwork for the scientific study of genetics and human inheritance with *The Origin of Species* in 1859 and *Expression of the Emotions in Man and Animals* in 1872. Concur-

[1] Esquirol, Jean-Etienne Dominique, *Des Maladies Mentales Considérées sous les Rapports Médical, Hygienique, et Médico-légal*, Accompagnées de Planches. J. B. Bailliere, Paris, 1838. 3 vols.

[2] *Ibid.*, vol. 2, p. 284. A translation.

rently with these developments, Francis Galton had become interested in his observation that eminent men are likely to have eminent sons.[1] His *Hereditary Genius* was published in 1869 and thereafter a series of treatises on human inheritance appeared which were to have profound influence upon scientific thinking. For the first time Galton made explicit the idea that human beings might differ radically in intelligence not only with respect to the distinction between being feebleminded and normal, but also at the other end of the scale. If it could be shown that innate differences in intelligence did exist, and there was evidence to suggest that such differences correlated with achievement in later life, then this immediately raised the possibility of predicting adult performance from some measure of innate ability in childhood, and at the very least, of predicting success on a job before hiring the candidate.

With the growing realization on the part of scientists and others interested in human behavior that the notion of innate intellectual differences between individuals could contribute much to the solution of the problem of predicting adult achievement, the stage was set for the second major development affecting the process of evaluating individual abilities: the invention of systematic techniques of measurement. Here, too, Galton played a dominant role.

By 1848 Quételet had discovered that probability theory could be applied to the physical measurements of human beings, and that the frequency distribution of such measurements corresponded closely to what we today call the normal curve. For example, the heights of a large group of men tend to cluster around an average, with observations becoming rarer and rarer the farther away from the average one moves in either direction. Galton went on to suggest that in addition to the absolute size of an object (for example, Smith is six feet one inch tall), its size relative to the size of other objects in the same class (Smith is 13 inches taller than the average man in the group) and the frequency of occurrence of observations of this magnitude (only one per cent of the men in this group are more than one foot

[1] Francis Galton, like Charles Darwin, was a grandson of Erasmus Darwin, who was one of the first to suggest the idea of inherited variation among human beings.

away from the average, that is, shorter than four feet or taller than six feet) are important facts.

This insight opened up new dimensions in measurement. With these conceptual tools, it became possible to evaluate individual abilities (for example, intelligence) by measuring the relative standing of the individual in a population of other individuals even though it was impossible to establish a zero point on the scale of measurement (for example, what constitutes zero intelligence). As knowledge about the properties of frequency distributions increased, it was possible to say, with some precision, for example, how much better or worse Johnnie had done on the test than Mary. In addition, through the use of probability theory one could say whether the difference between two persons' scores could reasonably have been expected to occur by chance if their abilities were in fact equal.

In addition to this concept of measurement expressed in terms of deviation from a norm or average, Galton also contributed the idea of correlation, which was later systematized by his protégé and colleague, Karl Pearson. The invention of a way to measure relationships between two sets of measurements, such as height and weight, or test score and academic grade averages, made it possible to find out systematically what test performance might mean in terms of any actual behavioral criterion one wanted to consider. It now became possible to evaluate a test instrument in terms of its value as a predictor of some later performance such as academic achievement and also to evaluate responses to particular questions within the test in terms of their empirical correlation with the overall test score.

By the turn of the century, most of the necessary elements were present for the introduction of systematic ways of measuring intellectual ability. The revolutionary concept of hereditary differences between human beings and the development of fundamental statistical techniques set the stage for the inventions of Binet, Thorndike, Terman, and Otis.

THE FIRST TESTS

Throughout the latter half of the nineteenth century, concurrently with the developments in statistics and genetics, work on the actual measurement of individual ability differences was under way in several places. Galton himself experimented with specific techniques for comparing individuals with respect to intellectual ability, most of them involving sensorimotor measurements of reaction time, perceptual acuity, and the like. In the United States Cattell also was making inferences about the presence of complex intellectual abilities from performance on simple motor tasks.[1]

A different approach, however, was taken by Alfred Binet and his followers in France, and it was Binet's work which was to lead directly to the development of the Binet-Simon scale of intelligence, the forerunner of present-day individual intelligence tests, and ultimately to the concept of "intelligence quotient." Binet wanted to measure abilities by presenting problems which required the use of the ability one was interested in measuring. As Goodenough points out, "In a word, they [Binet and his colleagues] were in favor of approaching the whole question of mental measurement by means of a sampling technique."[2]

Binet and his colleague Theodore Simon had for some time been observing the developmental sequences of children in terms of the tasks which they were progressively able to handle. In 1905 Binet and Simon devised a scale for the measurement of intelligence in which, for the first time, the tasks were arranged in order of difficulty rather than according to similarity or dissimilarity.[3]

This scale and subsequent revisions in 1908 and 1911 were translated into English by Goddard and formed the basis for Lewis Terman's 1916 Stanford revision. This was the first actual standardized test of intelligence. The 1916 Stanford-Binet, as it was called, was basically a new test with new items and a new scoring system, but its fundamental conception was in the tradition of Binet's original 1905 scale. It did, however, introduce the

[1] That the first efforts to isolate the referents of individual differences should be focused on physiological and simple motor skills is logical considering the long interest in such indicators of human ability. Goodenough points out that as early as the fourth century B.C., philosophers like Aristotle were attempting to discover the key to individual differences through physiological measurements.

[2] *Op. cit.*, p. 42.

[3] Goodenough notes that in 1887, Dr. S. E. Chaille had published a similar test in the *New Orleans Medical and Surgical Journal.* (*Op. cit.*, p. 50.) It is interesting to note that the scientific world was apparently not then ready for this innovation or perhaps we would be remembering the name Chaille instead of Binet.

notion of a ratio between mental age and chronological age (IQ) as a way of expressing test results. It was also the first test to have a series of well-organized and clear instructions for administering and scoring, two of the fundamental characteristics of a standardized test. The third requirement, norms based on a representative sample, was also met by Terman's test. The 1916 Stanford-Binet intelligence test enjoyed enormous popularity and remained in tremendous demand until 1937, when it was revised. The 1937 revision was made with considerable care and at the present time it is still the most widely used and prestigious individual test of intelligence.[1]

The Stanford-Binet test is an individual intelligence test, which means that it is administered to one person at a time by a trained psychologist. It also is primarily used with children. While its impact on the testing field has been enormous, and it is considered by many to be the most accurate measure of intelligence, relatively few children in our school systems have ever been given the Stanford-Binet test. This is due to the fact that only a trained person can administer the test, and it must be given individually.

The bulk of the standardized testing in the United States today in schools, in the civil service, in the military, and in industry is group testing. When we speak of standardized testing we typically mean objective, paper-and-pencil tests which are administered to a large group at one time. The Stanford-Binet test was only a beginning in the development of present-day standardized testing. The principles used in the formation of the 1916 scale were carried over into the creation of group tests of intelligence, achievement, and special aptitude, but the science of psychological measurement still had a long way to go in 1916.

THE DEVELOPMENT OF GROUP TESTING IN THE UNITED STATES

We have pointed out that in sociological terms, the appearance and acceptance of an innovation requires not only a favorable cultural climate and an adequate supporting technology or cultural base, but also the presence of relevant social needs which

[1] A 1960 revision was published by Houghton Mifflin Co. It is essentially a streamlining of the 1937 test.

serve to focus attention on the problem and ensure public acceptance of the new cultural product. The directions in which standardized testing has moved during the past forty years, the new forms of tests that have appeared, and the areas in which the public has been quick to accept testing on a large scale have been influenced by a variety of such social needs. These have resulted in some cases from gradual changes in American society and in other cases from major historical events. Among these trends and events we can distinguish the following: (1) World War I, with its influence on the development of group testing on a large scale, and World War II, which led to the growth of special aptitude testing; (2) prior to 1921, the problem of increasing numbers of immigrants who had to be absorbed by the society in a rational and maximally productive manner, which led to the development of nonverbal tests of intelligence; (3) following World War I, the increasing concern with public education in the context of growing emphasis on the traditional American values of equality of opportunity and encouragement of high achievement, which led to the growth of standardized achievement tests and further modifications of intelligence tests for school counseling and guidance uses; (4) the increasing technological complexity of the society throughout this period, which brought with it greater specialization of function and made necessary more efficient uses of manpower with respect to both training and allocation; and, finally, (5) the greater size and complexity of government, which produced a vast increase in the demands for civil servants and for equitable methods of selecting and promoting candidates for government service.

Group Testing in World Wars I and II

At the time the United States entered World War I, one of Terman's students, Arthur S. Otis, was bringing to completion his work on an intelligence test which could be administered simultaneously to a large number of individuals. The rapid buildup of a large army produced tremendous pressures for the development of a simple way of measuring the potential abilities of enlisted men and officer candidates. Otis was asked by a committee of the American Psychological Association to turn over his unpublished group intelligence test items to the Army. The result was the famous Army Alpha test which, in slightly modified form, is still widely used. The major success of the Army Alpha test as a predictor of performance paved the way for the introduction of group testing in education and in other areas where large numbers of individuals have to be classified quickly and efficiently.

With demobilization following World War I, military testing became relatively unimportant until the early 1940's, when once again the armed forces were faced with an emergency situation in which large numbers of men were being called into military service. World War II saw the development of the Army General Classification Test (AGCT) and following World War II, the Armed Forces Qualification Test (AFQT), which replaced it as a general screening test for draftees and men who were enlisting.

In 1940, however, war was more complex than in 1917. Several branches of the armed services, and in particular the Air Force, were confronted with the problem of selecting from a large number of candidates those men who were highly qualified for particularly difficult and specialized tasks. By this time psychologists had begun to conceive of human intelligence as composed of many special abilities or aptitudes. As the job requirements of pilots, navigators, and flight engineers became more clearly delineated, a new kind of screening device came into being—the battery of tests designed to provide a profile of aptitudes and abilities for each candidate. Early in World War II young men who qualified on the preliminary screening tests given by the Aviation Cadet Board were sent to Aircrew Classification Centers where they took twenty different aptitude classification tests. On the basis of their performance on these tests, they were assigned to pilot training or other schools appropriate to their special abilities. The value of these tests as predictors of the differential aptitudes required for the job of pilot, navigator, and bombadier was clearly reflected in the lower washout rates of men selected by these techniques as opposed to the old methods and they are still in use.

The Army followed suit with the creation of the Aptitude Area System shortly after World War II. This program consisted originally of a battery of nine special aptitude tests comprising the Army Classification Battery, which was administered to all inductees. The nine special aptitude tests included a Verbal Test, Arithmetic Reasoning Test, Pattern Analysis Test, Mechanical Aptitude Test, Army Clerical Speed Test, Army Radio Code Aptitude Test, Shop Mechanics Test, Automotive Information Test, and an Electronics Information Test. Various combinations of the scores on these tests were used to accomplish the classification of soldiers for occupational areas. In addition to the ACB, the Army now makes use of a large number of aptitude and achievement tests as screening devices in the selection of candidates for officer training, special service schools, and the like.

The use of standardized tests by the various branches of the armed forces both in World War I and World War II had a tremendous impact on the growth of testing throughout the society by providing clear demonstrations of the value of such techniques as screening devices and as predictors of high level performance in specialized positions. In addition to demonstrating the usefulness of general aptitude and intelligence tests, the Air Force Battery of special aptitude tests and later the Army Classification Battery have served to draw attention to the fact that intellectual abilities can most usefully be considered to be multidimensional rather than unidimensional as was first thought.[1]

Immigration and Nonverbal Tests of Intelligence

The Stanford-Binet and the Army Alpha were both verbal tests; that is, they were based in part on a measure of the subject's command of the English language. The person taking the Army Alpha had to be able to read the directions and questions, and also have a reasonably good vocabulary and knowledge of grammar in order to answer the questions correctly. However, the tremendous influx of immigrants prior to the enactment of the immigration laws of 1921 and 1924 made necessary the development of ability tests which could be given to non-English speaking

[1] It probably ought to be made clear here also that the development of multidimensional measurement techniques was based in part on the technological innovation of factor analysis and multiple correlation statistics, about which more will be said subsequently.

individuals in order to identify the feebleminded and others who would be unable to adapt readily to the society. In addition, there was a need for some way of measuring the intelligence of illiterate candidates for the armed services during World War I.

In 1914 H. A. Knox reported his work in testing mentally defective immigrants at Ellis Island, and while his tests were not well standardized, they formed the basis for the subsequent development of several "performance" tests. The first standardized nonverbal scale was published in 1917, only one year after the Stanford-Binet, by Pintner and Paterson. This was followed by the Army Beta test, which was the first group test designed for illiterates. The Army Beta turned out to have considerably lower reliability than the Army Alpha, and it is interesting to take note of the fact that up to the present time no one has succeeded in constructing a nonlanguage test that is as useful as the verbal tests in appraising general intelligence. The reason for this probably is that verbal ability is of critical importance in the performance of virtually every task requiring a high degree of intelligence and that therefore most of our criterion measures of intelligence contain a large verbal component.

Education and the Development of Standardized Achievement Tests

Although a considerable number of psychologists had been at work during the first two decades of the twentieth century on the development of standardized measures of academic achievement, it was not until after World War I that educators began seriously to consider the potentialities of standardized group achievement testing. E. L. Thorndike had written the first textbook on educational measurement, *An Introduction to the Theory of Mental and Social Measurement*, in 1904. Shortly thereafter, he and his students at Teachers College, Columbia University, devised the first achievement tests in arithmetic, handwriting, spelling, and other basic academic areas.

> These early workers in the measurement of achievement carried over from the psychological laboratory an awareness of the importance of carefully controlled administration and uniform scoring. They also took with them the statistical methodology that had been

> growing up in connection with the measurement of mental traits and applied it with ingenuity and effectiveness to the examination of achievement. Underscoring their efforts was a series of experiments that revealed the gross unreliability of the grading of the old type essay examination and the previously unsuspected extent to which students' marks on such tests were dependent upon the whims and prejudices of the teacher or the scorer.[1]

Once testing technology existed, large-scale applications of that technology in education depended on two factors. The first was the demonstration by the Army of the usefulness of standardized testing methods during World War I. The second was the important changes that were taking place in American educational philosophy and practice at the same time that larger numbers of students were entering high school. Not only was public education coming in for closer attention on the part of professional educators and the general population, but the trend was toward the development of a science of education and the use of scientific techniques in the improvement of instruction, guidance, and administration.

Given this orientation, the emerging recognition of the existence of ability differences between individuals and the traditional cultural emphasis on the opportunity for advancement led automatically in the direction of increasingly individualized instruction, differentiation of curriculum goals for different kinds of students, and, in general, a new focus on the problem of maximum realization of each individual's potentialities.

These developments in education led in turn to the use of standardized tests in the evaluation of pupil abilities and achievements. Tests became an increasingly popular means for selecting high and low ability students for special instruction at all levels within the educational system. Private schools and colleges found that scholastic aptitude and achievement tests answered their needs for some method of screening the increasing numbers of applicants according to their ability to compete at high levels of achievement. With the increasing selectivity and competition for college and university admission particularly since World War II, along with the appearance of vocational and other special pur-

[1] Lennon, Roger T., *Standardized Testing:* An Adventure in Educational Publishing. World Book Co., New York, 1955, p. 5.

pose schools, it became necessary for elementary and secondary schools to spend more and more time in guidance activities. Here again, tests proved to be of great assistance in adding to the counselor's file of information about a particular student.

A traditional and jealously guarded characteristic of American education has been the freedom of local school systems to set standards and decide upon matters of curriculum, grading, and teaching methods. The resulting diversity of background which is characteristic of American high school graduates has long been considered to be a strong point of American education, but it has also created some serious problems for college admissions directors and other officials who have had to make comparisons between students who may come from schools with different grading systems and different course requirements. Standardized tests have provided a solution to these problems by making possible the comparisons between students with widely divergent backgrounds on a set of standardized and uniform measures of ability and achievement. The fact that agencies such as the College Entrance Examination Board have made wide use of standardized tests[1] and have been among the leaders in the development of more reliable, valid measures of ability and achievement, serves to emphasize again the intimate relationship between the needs of the society and the acceptance and utilization of an innovation by the members of the society.

The rapid growth of educational testing has no doubt been spurred by the entrance of an increasingly large number of commercial publishers into the business of developing and distributing intelligence and achievement tests. The 1916 Stanford-Binet was published by Houghton Mifflin Company, and immediately following World War I, Otis was commissioned by the World Book Company to develop an educational testing program. These two publishers were soon joined by a large number of publishers and distributors, of which the most important today are probably the California Test Bureau, Science Research Associates,

[1] Largely as a result of the work of Carl Campbell Brigham, one of the pioneers in the development of standardized tests, the College Board decided to construct a scholastic aptitude test for use in college admissions in April of 1925. The test which resulted from this decision has evolved directly into the present College Board Tests: the Scholastic Aptitude Test and Scholastic Achievement Tests.

Inc., the Psychological Corporation, and the nonprofit Educational Testing Service. The competition among test publishers thus far has been based primarily on service and quality, with the result that tests have been improved, publishers have absorbed the high costs of standardization, and a relatively high degree of integrity has been maintained. An important reason for this record has been the policy of the leading publishers to rely heavily on qualified psychologists and testing specialists in the construction and standardization of new test instruments.

It is also likely that the test publishers have had much to do with speeding up the introduction of machine scoring and tabulating techniques into testing fields. In turn, these techniques have made possible more sophisticated statistical analyses of test scores and consequently more useful information for schools, admissions officials, and guidance counselors.

Testing in a Complex Society: Industry and Government

The twentieth century has witnessed the most remarkable outpouring of scientific knowledge and resulting technological advance in the history of the world. Industrial growth has been based in part on an ever-increasing division of labor and specialization of function. This growing complexity and specialization has brought with it new problems in the training and allocation of manpower within the society in order to ensure maximum utilization of resources. As the demand has grown, competition for the scarce resources of high ability and specialized talent (particularly in engineering and science fields) has forced private and public enterprise alike to look for new means of identifying and encouraging individuals with high ability.

In response to the growing problems of manpower allocation and selection, the personnel department in industry and the civil service administration in government have become important arbiters of positions within the society. Increasing numbers of jobs at all levels of American society are filled through the efforts of these two agencies. The chief tool of both the personnel man in industry and the Civil Service system in government has been the standardized test. The origin of testing on a large scale in government and industry also goes back to the years immediately following World War I.

During the decade 1920 to 1930 it is probable that the demand for tests and for qualified specialists to construct, administer, and interpret tests exceeded the supply by a considerable margin. Both industrial testing and civil service testing began with relatively simple tests designed to select workers for clerical and other low-level positions within the organization. Although the United States Civil Service had been using "competitive examinations" since the early 1870's when Grant's Secretary of the Interior, Jacob Dolson Cox issued a departmental order under which appointments to the Patent Office, Census Bureau, and Indian Office were to be made on the basis of such examinations, research on testing procedures and the use of standardized tests did not begin until the early 1920's.[1] By 1930, however, a wide range of tests had been developed and standardized (for example, the qualifying test for apprenticeship to mechanical trades in the navy yards) and civil service research activities were being carried forward on a variety of fronts. Civil service testing has continued to increase in extent and complexity along with the growth of government agencies at all levels, federal, state, and local. The present state of testing by government agencies will be examined in Chapter V.

As in the case of education, industrial testing was influenced by the entrance of commercial testing agencies into the field. In 1921 the Psychological Corporation was founded in New York for the purpose of applying psychological principles and techniques (most notably in the field of measurement) to the solution of industrial, educational, and social problems. It acted both as a distributor of tests published by such firms as the World Book Company and as a publisher in its own right. Many industrial firms were quick to take advantage of the services offered by such commercial test agencies. By 1960 a Harvard Business School Survey[2] indicated that better than 60 per cent of the

[1] Kavruck, Samuel, "Thirty-three Years of Test Research: A Short History of Test Development in the U. S. Civil Service Commission," *American Psychologist*, vol. 2, July, 1956, pp. 329–333.

[2] Ward, Lewis B., "Putting Executives to the Test," *Harvard Business Review*, vol. 38, July-August, 1960, pp. 6 ff.

very largest companies, those having more than 10,000 employees, were making regular use of tests in the selection of salaried personnel. Officials of the Psychological Corporation report that more than 90 per cent of the 600 largest companies in the country have purchased their tests at one time or another in the last decade.

Testing in industry has had its ups and downs. Organized labor has influenced testing in quite varied ways, which will be discussed in more detail in subsequent chapters. In general, however, unions have insisted on testing practices in those employment areas that are subject to political influence (for example, the Postal Workers Union) and have resisted testing, with considerable success, in nongovernment industries where testing has represented a threat to union control over hiring and firing. Management has tended to blow hot and cold on the use of tests in the selection of executive personnel and occasionally has compromised by writing its own tests which typically have not been standardized. It is probably safe to say that increasing numbers of standardized tests are being used at all levels of industry and in particular in those areas where special abilities and aptitudes are required.

AN INTERNATIONAL COMPARISON — RUSSIA AND GREAT BRITAIN

With the exception of Great Britain, the home of Galton and Pearson, the rest of the world has been slow to follow the example set by the United States in regard to the large-scale use of standardized tests. The reasons for this reluctance range from basic ideological and cultural differences of opinion about the nature of human abilities to technical and social problems which make the large-scale use of objective tests either difficult or impractical. We pointed out above that the acceptance of objective testing in the United States was a consequence of a variety of cultural and social factors in combination with the rapid development of statistical and other techniques necessary for test standardization. The importance of each of these factors in the growth of testing can be demonstrated even more clearly by a comparison of the testing practices in the United States, Russia, and England.

Testing in Russia

Because testing directly concerns the nature of human abilities, it is to be expected that the way a society views the abilities of its members will influence its attitudes toward testing and tests. This relationship is demonstrated by the divergent approaches to the evaluation and cultivation of human abilities manifested by Russia and Great Britain, and the resulting differences in beliefs about standardized tests. The principal disagreement between Russia and the West is over the contribution of inherited abilities to performance. Russian psychologists and educators have maintained, at least publicly, that differences in abilities between individuals are not the result of inherited factors; rather they are almost entirely a result of motivation, the efficacy of the teaching to which the individual has been exposed, and consequently his learning. The result has been a vehement disparagement by Soviet experts of anything resembling an intelligence or aptitude test purporting to contain a measure of an individual's innate potential.[1] According to one spokesman, "Soviet psychology rejects the pseudo-scientific pretension to measure ability or talent in any form and considers its main tasks to be the analysis of qualitative characteristics of aptitude and the discovery of methods for the successful development of abilities."[2] Selection among candidates for more advanced training does occur in the Soviet Union, however, and some testing, consisting primarily of essay and oral examinations, is carried on. The significant difference is that while in the United States and Britain, attempts are made to predict future performance on the basis of aptitude test scores, Russian educators have concentrated on evaluating past performance.

> If we [the Soviets] reject the method of tests and measurements, does this mean that we do not think it is necessary to investigate the abilities of the pupils? No, we do not believe this. But we hold that a correct investigation of abilities is possible only if the child's activities

[1] Tests were used in Russia, however, prior to the early 1930's. For a history of Soviet psychology, see Bauer, Raymond A., *The New Man in Soviet Psychology*, Harvard University Press, Cambridge, Mass., 1952.

[2] Smirnov, A. A., "The Development of Soviet Psychology" in *Soviet Psychology. A Symposium*. Philosophical Library, New York, 1961, p. 21.

are performed under his ordinary conditions of life, and when his abilities are not investigated statistically, but in their development and change, in connection with the whole personality of the child, his instruction and education, his entire life.[1]

Smirnov goes on to suggest that this process of evaluation is most appropriately left to the teacher, who is able to draw on extensive knowledge of the child's behavior under a variety of conditions. While in the United States the tendency has been to move in just the opposite direction, largely because of the many studies which have demonstrated the unreliability of teacher judgments, Russian educators have not hesitated to place considerable faith in such estimates.

Instead of concentrating on finding ways of differentiating among students of varying abilities, Russian educators have focused their efforts on developing the most efficient means of raising the total educational level of the society. Toward this end, all pupils in all Russian schools, whether a regular ten-year school, an evening school, a technical school, or some other specialized institution, are required to take the same general educational program, which at the secondary level is roughly equivalent to a basic college preparatory high school curriculum in this country. Henry Chauncey, president of the Educational Testing Service, following a visit to Russia with a team of American educators in 1957, reported that "the Russians believe that this basic academic education is good for all students except perhaps the 1% who may be mentally defective. They claim that they can get virtually all of their youth through such a program, and at the same time provide vocational training of all kinds. Their goal is to educate a vast reserve of young people who can take specialized training immediately or later on—as the need arises, and the state sees fit."[2] While many doubt that the Russian educational system is actually achieving this goal, there is evidence that in some areas a substantial majority of Russia's young people complete the program successfully. High motiva-

[1] *Ibid.*, p. 25.

[1] Chauncey, Henry, "Report of the President" in *Annual Report, 1957–1958*, Educational Testing Service, Princeton, N. J., 1958, p. 24.

tion on the part of students and teachers, as well as continuous efforts of Soviet psychologists and educators to improve teaching methods, have contributed to the success the program has achieved.

The Soviet view of human nature and the rejection of predictive ability tests is, of course, closely related to the political ideology of communism. In the published view of Russian observers, tests are used in capitalist countries primarily in order to serve "political, reactionary class aims."[1] According to Smirnov, "such tests are used to prove that the level of ability is lower in children of workers and peasants than in children of the propertied classes, and that the abilities of children of subject peoples are lower than those of children of the so-called 'higher' peoples and 'higher' races. These tests serve as foundation for the assertion that social inequality is based on and justified by such differences of aptitude."[2] He goes on to state the Russian position that the correlation between IQ scores and class position is due to the fact that members of the various classes differ in their access to the educational opportunities of the society. "If, in capitalist countries, the children of workers achieve worse results in tests than the children of property owners, it is not because they are less gifted but because they were greatly hampered in developing their abilities by their conditions of life, determined by the oppression, exploitation and social and economic inequality prevailing in these countries."[3]

In the light of these statements, the Soviet position on testing is not surprising. Despite substantial empirical evidence that inherited differences in intellectual and other abilities do play an important role in performance, the Russians have elected to reject completely the concept of "talent discovery" and substitute instead that of "talent development." In addition to providing grist for the Soviet propaganda mill, such a view of human ability is not without merit on its own terms. We have much evidence that class groups within a society frequently do form distinctive subcultures which are likely to influence the per-

[1] Smirnov, A. A., *op. cit.*, p. 24.

[2] *Ibid.*

[3] *Ibid.*

formance of their members on ability tests.[1] Moreover, it is possible that a completely achievement-oriented educational system leads to greater overall motivation on the part of students and teachers alike. This issue will be discussed in more detail in a later chapter, but it may be observed here that the relative contribution of environmental and genetic factors to performance remains an open question. Russian efforts to raise the general educational level of the population appear to have had significant results. It will be interesting to see whether the present achievement level can be maintained or advanced as the number of candidates for advanced training increases.

Testing in Great Britain

While testing theory and practice in the United States have followed a middle course, with an admission on our part that both the environment and genetic background are important in the evaluation of abilities, the British have tended to place more emphasis on the contribution of inheritance. In addition to the fact that the early work on inheritance and intelligence was done in England by Darwin, Galton, and others, Great Britain has long been characterized by a fairly rigid class structure, based in large part on inherited privileges. Although the structure of British society has been changing during the past several decades, the vestiges of this tradition still exert a strong influence throughout the society. It is doubtful that anyone in Great Britain holds the extreme position of genetic determinism, but the long-term interest of the British in the genetic component in performance has led to a somewhat greater preoccupation with ways of measuring intelligence and the possibilities of improving the general level of intelligence of the population as a whole through selective breeding. A case in point is Cyril Burt's statement that "improved environmental amenities can of themselves ensure no lasting results; but the changes in a nation's genetic constitution are likely to prove irreversible."[2] The interest in the genetic bases

[1] Charters, W. W., Jr., "Social Class and Intelligence Tests" in Charters, W. W., Jr., and N. L. Gage, editors, *Readings in the Social Psychology of Education*, Allyn and Bacon, Inc., Boston, 1963, pp. 12–21.

[2] Burt, Cyril, "The Inheritance of Mental Ability," *American Psychologist*, vol. 13, January, 1958, p. 9.

of intelligence has led to a heavier dependence on intelligence and aptitude test scores as predictors of an individual's future performance.

The most widely publicized and frequently discussed example of the use of standardized tests in Great Britain is the examination for admission to grammar school (college preparatory secondary school), which typically occurs at age eleven. Prior to the passage of the Education Act of 1944, the opportunity for education beyond the primary grades was restricted to a selected few, not always in direct proportion to their ability. However, the British have since accepted the ideal of universal secondary education and have worked hard to implement this policy by providing additional educational facilities and by encouraging children to remain in school longer. Four thousand new schools have been built within the past two decades, the number of trained teachers has been raised by 85,000 (to 260,000) since the war, and the school population has increased by over a quarter. In 1947 the minimum school leaving age was raised to fifteen for all children and the number staying in school voluntarily beyond this age has increased more than 50 per cent, from 187,000 in 1948 to 290,000 in 1958.[1]

The function of providing educational facilities is delegated to the 146 Local Education Authorities in England and Wales. These Authorities are free to plan the local system of education as they wish, provided that the educational opportunities afford all pupils with "such variety of instruction and training as may be desirable in view of their different ages, abilities and aptitudes."[2] As a result of this local autonomy, educational opportunities, practices, and methods of selection vary considerably, just as they do in the United States. All children attend elementary school until age eleven (corresponding to completion of the fifth grade in the United States), at which time they normally enter one of four different types of secondary school, depending on the practice in their school district. The two most frequently encountered types of public secondary school are the grammar schools

[1] *Secondary Education for All:* A New Drive. A Pamphlet Presented to Parliament by the Minister of Education by Command of Her Majesty, December, 1958.

[2] *Selection for Secondary Education in England and Wales*, ID 1312. Mimeographed, available free on request from British Information Services, New York.

and the secondary modern schools. Grammar schools provide a largely academic curriculum leading to the GCE, or General Certificate of Education examinations, which are prerequisite to university entrance. Secondary modern schools include more vocational subjects, home economics training for girls, and a basic academic curriculum designed primarily for children who will be leaving school at age fifteen. In addition to grammar and secondary modern schools, students in some areas have the opportunity to enter a secondary technical school, which is like a grammar school with a bias toward scientific and practical subjects. Others may enter a comprehensive school offering both academic and vocational subjects. Comprehensive schools, the newest development in British education, are usually larger (often enrolling 1,000 to 2,000 students); they enroll children at all levels of intelligence, and they closely resemble the standard American public high school.

Most local education authorities provide separate secondary schools for children of different abilities, and "since, by and large, the alternative forms of secondary education available have not yet earned the prestige that grammar schools enjoy, the transfer of pupils from primary to secondary schools has come to be regarded as one of the most decisive stages in a child's educational career. If he is given a place in a grammar school (or secondary technical school), he tends to be regarded as a 'success'; if he is allocated to a secondary modern school, for example, he is often dubbed a 'failure.'"[1] Grammar schools typically accommodate from 12 per cent to 15 per cent of the child population, depending on the financial resources of the Local Authority;[2] and it is in the selection of this relatively small group of children that standardized, objective tests play a major role. Because the children in primary schools due to be transferred to secondary schools are those who will have reached the age of eleven by the first of September, the entrance examination

[1] Yates, A., and Pidgeon, D. A., *Admission to Grammar Schools:* Third Interim Report. Publication No. 10 of the National Foundation for Educational Research in England and Wales, Newnes, 1957. The authors go on to note that "even if the use of such terms (as 'success' or 'failure') is eschewed by authorities, teachers, and parents, it appears to be not uncommon for the children themselves to use them in describing the outcome of the process of allocation." (p. 175).

[2] *Selection for Secondary Education in England and Wales*, ID1312.

for grammar school is commonly referred to as the "eleven-plus" examination.[1]

Just as there are differences between local authorities with respect to the availability of grammar school openings, there is also some variation in the selection procedure used to fill these places. Virtually all the authorities, however, use objective tests and nine out of ten, an IQ test. The predominant pattern is a combination of an intelligence test and standardized achievement tests in English and arithmetic. Usually, a merit ranking based on the combined test scores of the children is compiled and the top 12 to 15 per cent of the children (depending on the number of places available) are assigned to grammar school. In borderline cases the recommendation of the "primary head" or elementary school principal is also considered.

It is not surprising that this procedure has caused considerable controversy and much anxiety on the part of parents and children alike. In effect, the British have advanced by five or six years the critical choice point which occurs during college admissions in the United States. Because the child who fails to get into grammar school has considerably less opportunity to receive an academic secondary education leading to university entrance, the "eleven-plus" examination becomes the functional equivalent of our College Board test, albeit at a much earlier age. Furthermore, there are far fewer alternatives open to a child who does poorly on the eleven-plus examination than to a high school student who does poorly on the Scholastic Aptitude Test of the College Board. In the United States, the student may take the SAT again, or apply to a college that does not require SAT scores (for example, most state universities). In England, the child who misses out on grammar school admission may sometimes get into an academic curriculum leading to the GCE examinations in a secondary modern school, but he knows that the odds are against his performing as well on this high level achievement test as his

[1] Actually, this is something of a misnomer since the ages of children taking the examination may range from 10 years and 6 months to 11 years and 5 months. Test scores, however, are standardized into a scale which takes into account the child's exact age.

Not all eleven-year-olds are permitted to take the selection examination. Usually between 66 per cent and 98 per cent of the children enrolled in primary schools are tested, depending on the local authority.

competitors who have had the advantage of a grammar school education.

The transition from primary to secondary school is not the only point at which standardized tests are used by the British, but it provides the best example of the differences existing among Russia, the United States, and Great Britain. The British have thus far taken the position that it is possible, through the use of objective tests, to obtain a sufficiently accurate measure of potential ability at a relatively early age, to warrant a critical selection of children based on test scores at age eleven.

It is apparent that the United States and Britain have provided environments uniquely suited to the rapid development and widespread utilization of testing technology. These comparisons serve to emphasize not only the magnitude of the testing industry here in the United States, but in addition, some of the cultural and social differences between this country and the rest of the world. They also raise some interesting questions about the future of the testing movement, both in this country and abroad; for example, what part can testing be expected to play in the current struggle for international power and prestige between the United States and Russia? Some of the implications of testing for American society will be examined in Chapter VIII.

SUMMARY

We have noted that standardized ability testing has become widespread in the United States during the past fifty years, and that until recently it has been a uniquely American phenomenon. The rapid growth of testing in this society can be traced to a combination of cultural forces which culminated in the early 1920's in the beginnings of extensive group testing by the military, educational institutions, government, and industry. In addition to the development of the necessary statistical and methodological technology, to which such pioneers as Galton, Binet, Terman, Thorndike, and Otis contributed, the acceptance by the society of this innovation was dependent upon several factors. The most important cultural change which contributed both to the development of systematic measures of ability and to their popular acceptance was the realization that inherited differences in intelligence and other abilities did exist between individuals. This revelation focused attention on the problem of developing ways to measure these differences; and in combination with the traditional American values of achievement and mobility, it provided the groundwork for the resulting shift from the old ways of assigning status in the society (family background, race, and so on) toward this new criterion: performance on a standardized test of ability.

The speed of the transition was influenced strongly by the course of events in the early part of the twentieth century. The manpower allocation problems created by World War I and World War II, the influx of immigrants prior to 1921, the growing concern with the efficiency of our system of public education beginning in the 1920's, the increasing technological complexity of the society which made necessary better ways of identifying talented individuals to fill the specialized requirements of new jobs, and the extraordinary growth of government which has created large civil service manpower requirements have all had important effects on the growth of the testing movement. In response to these social needs and the resulting demands for a testing technology, commercial test publishers and distributors have taken over a large part of the responsibility for the development of accurate instruments and they have in turn had the effect of increasing the demand for tests.

Our survey of the historical background of the testing movement has dealt primarily with the social and cultural factors in the growth of testing. We have intentionally neglected many details, such as who developed a particular test in what year. Instead, we have tried to set the development of the testing movement in its proper cultural perspective. In the following chapters we will attempt to evaluate the current status of the testing movement and its implications for the society.

III

An Overview of Ability Testing Today

NO ONE KNOWS WITH CERTAINTY how many standardized tests are being given every year, what proportion of the population is being or has been tested, or precisely what use is made of the scores that result. The impression, which is supported by sales figures from commercial test publishers, anguished pleas from school administrators for a reduction in the number of external testing programs, the frequency of announcements of Civil Service examinations in newspapers, and the growing number of test coaching courses, is that testing has become a major activity in American society, and that test scores are playing an increasingly important role in decisions about people. The facts, however, are fragmented and often obscured by conjecture and emotion. While data gathered from a variety of sources may permit us to make some educated guesses about the extent of testing in the society, the uses to which the resulting test scores are put remain a major source of confusion. It is extremely difficult to evaluate the importance of standardized testing in college admissions, industrial employment or even military manpower allocation, particularly in those cases where actual practice may vary considerably from public pronouncement and formally established procedure. Indeed, there is evidence which suggests that frequently even those individuals who are directly involved in making use of test scores are not aware of how much or how little they rely on an individual's score in making decisions.[1]

An estimate of the extent of testing and the way test scores are being used must be made, however, if we are to evaluate the impact that testing is having on the society. The following two

[1] Hastings, J. Thomas, and others, *The Use of Test Results*. Bureau of Educational Research, Urbana, Ill., 1960.

chapters represent an attempt to make some sense out of the fragmentary information available on the amount of testing being done in this country and to summarize what is known about the way tests are used. As was pointed out above, the data were obtained from published statements by individuals and organizations in the field of standardized testing and by major users of tests, and from extensive interviews with psychometricians, school administrators, government officials, and independent observers on the testing scene. What emerges is a necessarily incomplete image of current practice and an indication of possible trends on which projections into the future might be based.

HOW MANY TESTS HAVE BEEN DEVELOPED?

In 1961 Oscar Buros compiled a comprehensive bibliography of tests in print which included 2,126 separate entries, each representing a different test or test battery. See Table 1. Included

TABLE 1. IN-PRINT TESTS BY MAJOR CLASSIFICATIONS[a]

Classification	Number of entries	Percentage of entries
Character and Personality	306	14.4
Vocations	287	13.5
Intelligence	238	11.2
Miscellaneous	233	11.0
Mathematics	198	9.3
English	192	9.0
Reading	159	7.5
Social Studies	113	5.3
Science	106	5.0
Foreign Languages	92	4.3
Sensory-Motor	55	2.6
Business Education	53	2.5
Achievement Batteries	45	2.1
Fine Arts	29	1.4
Multi-aptitude Batteries	20	0.9
Total	2,126	100.0

[a] Buros, Oscar Krisen, editor, *Tests in Print*. The Gryphon Press, Highland Park, N.J., 1961, p. xix.

in this compilation are tests of intelligence, achievement, character and personality, vocational interest, and special abilities such as etiquette, handwriting, and listening comprehension. The bulk of these tests fall under the general heading achievement tests, while personality and intelligence tests make up the bulk of the remainder. In 1939 Hildreth[1] compiled a bibliography of psychological tests covering the preceding fifty-year period in which some four thousand different tests were listed. This listing was updated in 1945 with the addition of approximately a thousand new titles. It is likely that all of these lists together are still far from complete, since an increasing number of private and public organizations develop their own tests which never find their way into a reviewer's hands or a bibliographical listing. Into this latter category fall the standardized tests developed by such organizations as the U.S. Civil Service Commission, the New York City public school system, the Army, Navy, and Air Force, and the New York State Board of Regents, as well as the various *ad hoc*, semi-standardized tests being given by industrial personnel departments throughout the country. Even if we consider only intelligence and achievement measures (as opposed to personality, vocational interest, etiquette tests, and the like), a conservative estimate of the number of different standardized tests that have been used in the United States during the past half-century still runs into the thousands.

HOW ARE TESTS USED?

These tests have been and are being used for four general purposes: (1) as a basis for classification and placement, including academic admissions, hiring, and promotion, (2) as a basis for awards such as scholarships, (3) as a diagnostic technique in counseling and treatment, and (4) in research (typically evaluation of change). Most of the activities which come to mind when someone mentions testing fall into the first category, including college admissions, the College Board and American College Testing programs, military testing (for example, Army General Classification Test), Civil Service tests (for example, Federal Service Entrance Examination), and industrial testing. Standardized tests are also used for placing pupils in homogeneous groups or special sections for maximum teaching efficiency. It should be emphasized that usually the test scores are not the sole criterion in the classification process, but merely an additional bit

[1] Hildreth, Gertrude, *Bibliography of Mental Tests and Rating Scales*. The Psychological Corporation, New York, 1939. *Supplement*, 1945.

of information in the process of making decisions about an individual. It is this fact that leads to difficulties in evaluating the reliance placed on a test score. If the test score were the only thing used in making these decisions, it would be relatively easy to assess the role of testing in our society. However, many factors enter into the process of admissions, classification, and job assignment. Under these conditions, it often becomes extremely difficult to state with any certainty the extent to which tests influenced the final outcome of the decision process.

In addition to classification and placement, tests have been used increasingly in the process of granting scholarships and other awards indicative of achievement or promise. Many of the much criticized external testing programs imposed on high school students are for the purpose of selecting scholarship winners (for example, the National Merit Scholarship Qualifying Test), and frequently organizations desiring to give scholarships make use of scores on tests administered for other purposes (for example, Scholastic Aptitude Test scores). Again, the role played by the test score in the selection process varies, but in general, where the number of candidates is large in relation to the number of awards to be given, heavier reliance is likely to be placed on the test score, which is a more or less objective and easily applicable criterion. On the other hand, where the number of candidates is small and homogeneous, other factors may play a larger role.

Tests are also being used increasingly by guidance personnel in schools and by clinical psychologists in the treatment of character disorders of one kind or another. The use of tests by school personnel includes both guidance work at all levels with normal children who need help in evaluating their abilities in order to plan their future activities, and the treatment of personality problems of a more or less serious nature through psychological counseling. In addition to school guidance testing, an increasing number of employment agencies and executive counselors are making use of tests in the guidance of adults at all job levels. Clinical uses of standardized tests are quite varied, and are heavily weighted in the direction of personality tests and vocational interest inventories as opposed to what we have defined as ability tests. Since our principal concern is with the latter kind of tests, this discussion will be restricted primarily to the use of intelligence, aptitude, and achievement tests in guidance.

Finally, tests are frequently used as measures of the dependent variable in evaluative research. Examples of such usage would be the evaluation of changes in teaching methods or curriculum content through the use of achievement tests, or the evaluation of alternative counseling techniques through the use of personality tests.

It should be made clear that a single test or battery of tests might serve any or all of the preceding functions: classification, scholarship awards, counseling, and research. And, indeed, many tests do have multiple uses in schools and other organizations. A guidance counselor may make use of scores from a classification battery for purposes of advising students on their course selection and the principal may use the same set of scores for evaluating the efficacy of a new method of teaching or the performance of a given teacher.

WHAT ORGANIZATIONS USE TESTS?

Standardized tests are presently being used by virtually every large organization that carries on any of these activities: hiring or admission, classification, promotion, the awarding of scholarships, treatment, and evaluation of change. The biggest users of tests are, of course, educational institutions, but military and federal, state and local civil service testing have become increasingly important. The amount of testing done by government agencies and the branches of the armed services is frequently overlooked because these agencies develop their own tests for the most part[1] rather than purchase tests from commercial test publishers. In addition to schools, the government, and the military, tests are being used at various levels in industry in the selection of personnel and, to a lesser degree, in determining candidacy for promotion. Tests are also used extensively by state agencies in the classification of mentally retarded children and by custodial institutions, such as mental hospitals and prisons, in order to provide a basis for differential training and treatment.

[1] There are a few exceptions, for example, the Peace Corps, which uses the services of the Educational Testing Service for some aspects of candidate evaluation.

WHO MAKES TESTS?

In general, standardized tests are produced by three types of organizations. The profit-making commercial test publisher and the nonprofit testing service are the most visible and consequently the best-known sources of tests. Their products are also much more readily available and therefore directly and indirectly may affect greater numbers of people. The third source of tests is, as we have already suggested, those large organizations that develop tests for their own use. In this category we find the armed services, most civilian government agencies that make use of tests, a fair number of large public school systems or state departments of education, and many industrial firms that have either developed their own tests or modified existing tests for their purposes. As school systems, industrial firms, and government agencies have grown in size, private development and standardization of tests have become more practical from the standpoint of these test users. The result is that, in terms of the total number of tests administered annually, commercial and nonprofit test agencies are no longer the only significant source of published tests. This development is a subtle but important shift in the balance of power in the testing industry and one that has led commercial test publishers to stress the convenience of scoring services and the advantages of norms based on larger populations for comparison purposes.

Commercial and nonprofit testing services have been in the testing business from the beginning. Standardization of a test is a costly process and publishers have been willing to undertake these expenses in return for copyright and publishing rights. While the 900 odd tests reviewed in the *Fifth Mental Measurements Yearbook*[1] were published by more than 150 different organizations, the bulk of commercial test publishing is done by a small group of firms that hold the copyrights of the best-known tests. These companies frequently have distributor arrangements with smaller firms in addition to marketing their tests themselves. The profit-making companies that operate solely as publishers (that is, they do not distribute tests published by com-

[1] Buros, Oscar Krisen, editor, *Fifth Mental Measurements Yearbook.* The Gryphon Press, Highland Park, N.J., 1953.

petitors) include Houghton Mifflin Company, which holds the copyright on the Stanford-Binet intelligence test; Harcourt, Brace and World, Inc. (formerly the World Book Company), which holds the copyright on the Otis tests; the California Test Bureau, which publishes the California Test of Mental Maturity, among others; Science Research Associates, Inc., which produces the SRA Achievement Test series; and the Personnel Press, which publishes only one test, the Kuhlmann-Anderson Intelligence Test. The Psychological Corporation of New York operates both as a publisher (Wechsler-Bellevue IQ Test) and a distributor of tests published by other companies. The nonprofit Educational Testing Service of Princeton, New Jersey, occupies a preeminent position in the testing field, in part because of its connection with the College Entrance Examination Board. Another nonprofit organization, the Educational Records Bureau, provides test and evaluation services primarily for private secondary schools. There are, in addition, many other smaller nonprofit test publishers.

All of these test agencies and the twenty or so additional major test distributors issue catalogues that describe their tests and other products and services (for example, scoring and norming services), which are available to anyone. The American Psychological Association has formulated fairly explicit guidelines as to the professional qualifications necessary for potential test purchasers[1] and all reputable firms sell tests only to those individuals who are qualified to make proper use of them. Unfortunately, less scrupulous firms do exist, with the result that control over test distribution has remained a problem.

Each major test publisher, both profit and nonprofit, has tended to delineate its own areas of specialization in relation to the test-using public. California Test Bureau, Harcourt, Brace and World, Inc., and Science Research Associates, Inc., have traditionally been associated primarily with school testing. Science Research Associates has been heavily involved in the development of achievement test batteries and is at present responsible

[1] See *American Psychologist*, vol. 9, February, 1954, pp. 55–61; vol. 13, June, 1958, pp. 266–271; or *The Psychological Corporation Test Catalog, 1961*, The Psychological Corporation, New York, pp. 4–5.

for the tests used by the American College Testing Program and the National Merit Scholarship Program, among others. The Psychological Corporation has specialized in nonacademic testing and has been instrumental in the development of a variety of personality measures, as well as tests suitable for industrial personnel selection and high level performance evaluation. The Educational Testing Service, in addition to the development and administration of the highly respected College Board examinations, administers a variety of other national testing programs, including the Graduate Record Examination, the Law School Admissions Test, and the Peace Corps Entrance Tests. The Cooperative Test Division of ETS also publishes the well-known SCAT (School and College Ability Tests) and STEP (Sequential Tests of Educational Progress) series, along with a variety of other aptitude and achievement tests.

As mentioned above, many of the larger test publishers and distributors are concerned with the improvement of their products and most of them maintain a sizable staff of salesmen to assist test users in selecting the right test, administering it, and interpreting the results. Several agencies also publish research findings and public information pamphlets. In general, the commercial as well as the nonprofit publishers of standardized tests are aware of their responsibilities to the groups they serve, and they go to great lengths to improve public understanding of their activities and aims.

Groups that develop and administer their own tests, however, may vary considerably with respect to testing practices and policies. Some organizations like the Personnel Research Branch of the Army and the Civil Service Commission maintain a large capable staff of psychometricians, who are engaged in validation research and other work designed to improve the efficiency and accuracy of their tests. Other agencies may be forced, as a result of lack of funds or manpower, to make use of fairly crude techniques of test construction and validation, and the resulting instruments may not be subject to critical evaluation by impartial specialists as is usually the case for commercially marketed tests (for example, in issues of the *Mental Measurements Yearbook*).[1]

[1] See note, p. 50.

HOW MANY TESTS ARE GIVEN ANNUALLY?

Reliable estimates of the number of standardized tests being given annually in the United States are extraordinarily difficult to come by. Because, as we have noted, testing is carried on by so great a variety of organizations, with many different instruments and for various reasons, any precise tabulation would seem to be, at least for the present, out of the question. The problem is further compounded by the difficulty in deciding what to count as a single test. Some groups regard a battery of aptitude or achievement tests as a single test, others count each test in the battery as a separate test. Despite these differences, it is interesting to attempt a guess at the extent of testing based on the scattered data available.

The annual survey of standardized test publishers, which is conducted by the American Textbook Publishers Institute, tabulates test sales reports from 17 major test publishers (including all those mentioned above),[1] representing 93 per cent of the total over-the-counter sales in the testing industry. The most recent annual survey of the American Textbook Publishers Institute indicates that approximately 75 million test booklets, many of which contain their own answer sheet, and an additional 66 million separate answer sheets, having a total value of $11,490,000, were sold in 1961. The ATPI report also indicates the tremendous growth of testing during the past decade. The comparable data for 1954 showed combined sales of 82 million booklets and answer sheets, having a value of $5,420,000 or about half the dollar value of the 1961 sales. The figures for test booklets sold include both consumable and re-usable instruments, while it is assumed that all answer sheets are used for only one testing. These numbers include sales of personality tests, as well as those we have defined as ability tests. As a result of these complications,

[1] The Bobbs-Merrill Company; Martin M. Bruce; California Test Bureau; Columbia University, Teachers College, Bureau of Publications; Educational Records Bureau; Educational Testing Service, Cooperative Test Division; Harcourt, Brace and World, Inc.; Harlow Publishing Corporation; Houghton Mifflin Company; Kansas State Teachers College, Bureau of Educational Measurements; Ohio Scholarship Tests, Ohio State Department of Education; Personnel Press, Inc.; The Psychological Corporation; Purdue University, State High School Testing Service for Indiana; Science Research Associates, Inc.; State University of Iowa, Bureau of Educational Research; The Steck Company.

along with the fact that it is not known what proportion of tests sold are actually administered, it is difficult to evaluate the meaning of these figures. A conservative estimate based on this report, however, indicates that more than 100 million commercially produced ability tests were administered in 1961.

But these numbers, as large as they are, represent only part of the total picture. While the sales of the Cooperative Test Division of the Educational Testing Service are included in the annual survey, the more than two million tests administered by the College Board and General Programs Divisions of ETS are not included in the report. In New York State alone, the Regents Examination Program accounts for several million test administrations per year that do not appear in the ATPI figures, and the Bureau of Educational Research of the Board of Education of the City of New York has constructed and standardized several different tests that are administered to more than half a million public school children in New York City each year but do not appear on any summation of test sales. Many other states and several other large cities have comparable testing programs that are not tabulated anywhere.

Military personnel experts estimate that most members of the armed forces take more than one standardized test every year and frequently as many as 15 or 20. These figures have never been included in any summary of the extent of testing. Federal Civil Service testing accounts for an additional million tests administered each year, while state and local merit system testing adds another million or so. All of the above-mentioned testing activities are at least potentially countable, but industrial testing with homemade, semi-standardized instruments contributes an amount that is well-nigh impossible to measure.

In summary, it is probably safe to say that there are more ability tests being given annually in the United States than there are people. In the next two chapters, we will attempt to describe in somewhat greater detail the extent of testing in each of four major institutional areas of the society: education, industry, government, and the military.

IV

Testing in Education

THE USES OF STANDARDIZED ABILITY TESTS in schools and colleges generally fall into one of two categories: internal testing which is carried on within the school or college by the institution for purposes of its own, and external testing which may or may not take place in the school, but which is sponsored by outside organizations (often other schools) primarily for the benefit of the outside group. Some test results, of course, may be used by both an external agency and the school itself, but most of them can be classified by major purpose into one or the other of these two categories.

Much of the controversy that has surrounded testing in recent years has been focused on the pressures and problems created by external testing programs such as college entrance examinations, the scholarship award programs, and the state certification tests.[1] While these tests are more easily visible in impact and effect to parents and students, and thereby generate more controversy, the actual amount of testing done as a result of external testing programs is small relative to the extent of within-school testing, the bulk of which takes place at elementary-grade levels rather than in secondary schools. Many parents may not be aware of the frequency with which their children are exposed to standardized tests throughout the first eight or nine grades, nor do they realize the effects that scores on these earlier tests may have on subsequent educational experiences, up to and including the child's performance on the external tests he will face as a high school student. It is possible, for example, that a child who does poorly on aptitude tests in the first and second grades will be given less attention by the teacher, or placed in a slower section

[1] It should be pointed out that the pressures produced by the various testing programs are partly a reflection of the increased competition for college admission.

for instructional purposes, and, as a result, may have a substantially lowered chance of performing well on a college entrance examination ten years later. The self-fulfilling prophecy characteristics of ability tests are discussed in greater detail in Chapter VII. Here it should be noted that because they come first, internal testing programs may have as great, if not greater, impact on children and schools than the widely criticized external programs.

Tests are given by schools for various purposes, as already indicated. Goodenough points out that, essentially, "mental measurement in schools and colleges is designed to further the end toward which all education is directed—that of furnishing the best possible opportunity for the growth and development of the individual student."[1] The rationale for the use of tests in schools stems from the belief that if we are going to use scientific techniques in order to improve teaching, then we must know all there is to know about our pupils in order to utilize fully our new instructional methods. Educators have only quite recently come to realize that learning involves a process of interaction between the student and his environment, and that both parts of the equation are important—the needs and unique capabilities of the student, as well as the demands of the situation. From this point of view, new teaching methods are useless without information about the characteristics of the individuals on whom they are to be used. Theoretically, standardized tests are designed to provide some of the necessary information about pupils in a scientific way. Instead of measuring children with a yardstick that changes in length, depending on who is holding it—as may be the case where teacher ratings are relied upon—standardized tests make it possible to compare students on a scale that remains relatively constant. Although we may wish to question whether the units used are most appropriate, we at least have something that can be discussed systematically.

INTERNAL TESTING

How extensive is internal testing at the elementary, secondary, and college levels? What are the main objectives of internal

[1] Goodenough, Florence L., *Mental Testing*. Rinehart and Co., New York, 1949, p. 455.

testing programs? What individuals are primarily responsible for the selection, administration, and interpretation of results? Who pays for the tests and the scoring services? What agencies have been set up to assist schools in establishing testing programs and in making the best use of test results? What kinds of tests are predominantly used and who makes them? What does a "typical" testing program look like? What controls are there to ensure that test scores are not misused by counselors, administrators, parents, and others in a position to make decisions about the child? What is the general practice of schools and colleges with respect to the reporting of test scores to students and their parents? These are some of the important questions that can be asked about current testing practices in education. While the answers to all of them cannot be given in minute detail, an attempt will be made to evaluate the evidence we do have.

Extent of Internal Testing

According to the best estimates of educational test publishers and the empirical data available from studies of testing practices in a few states, it appears that somewhere between 75 per cent and 90 per cent of all public elementary and secondary school systems in the United States make use of standardized tests at least once between kindergarten and grade 12. The frequency of test use, however, varies considerably according to the size of the school, financial resources available, urban versus rural locale, region of the country, and the inclination of school administrators. All of the Class A (largest) school systems in a recent survey of testing practices in Michigan[1] used tests regularly, while only 74 per cent of the Class D (smallest) systems had a testing program. In New England a study by Winston Keck[2] indicated that virtually all the school systems tabulated made use of tests, but that there was considerable variation in the extent of the program according to size of system and financial resources.

Data on the use of standardized tests in a sample of over 800 public senior high schools were collected in 1960 in connection

[1] Womer, Frank B., *Testing Programs in Michigan Schools.* A Study Conducted by the Testing and Guidance Committee. Michigan Association of Secondary School Principals, University of Michigan, 1959.

[2] Keck, Winston, "Testing and Evaluation Practices in New England Public Schools." Unpublished doctoral dissertation, Boston University, 1961.

with Project Talent, a national inventory of aptitudes and abilities presently being carried out by the University of Pittsburgh.[1] According to John T. Dailey, program director, nearly all the schools sampled reported that they made use of standardized tests or inventories.[2] Only southeastern rural schools and schools located in lower socioeconomic neighborhoods in the urban Southeast, Midwest, and West reported less than 95 per cent use of tests. More than 90 per cent of the schools indicated that their counseling and testing services had been increased in recent years, and that they were making greater (and more effective) use of standardized tests. Despite the present extent of testing, an overwhelming majority of the schools replied that they plan to increase the scope of their testing programs.

The high schools participating in Project Talent were divided into 17 homogeneous groups based on housing quality (socioeconomic status), region, and rural-urban status.[3] Table 2 shows the number of schools in each of these categories and Figure 1 presents data on the percentage of schools using paper IQ tests (group tests), individual IQ tests, and multiple aptitude test batteries, by type of school. It is interesting to note the relative frequency of use of individual IQ tests in northeastern urban high-cost housing schools as compared with rural and town schools. Also of interest is the curiously low incidence of multiple aptitude testing in vocational high schools. Dailey points out that "it would seem that these would be just the schools where multiple aptitude batteries would be of most value."[4]

Some states, however, exceed even these fairly high rates of testing. In 1960 a study of testing practices in California[5] revealed

[1] Project Talent is being conducted jointly by the University of Pittsburgh and the American Institute for Research, with the support of the United States Office of Education and with assistance from the National Institute of Mental Health, the National Science Foundation, and the Office of Naval Research. Dr. John C. Flanagan is the Responsible Investigator.

[2] Dailey, John T., "A Survey of the Use of Tests in Public High Schools." Paper presented at the Twelfth Annual Conference of Directors of State Testing Programs at Princeton, N. J., November 4–5, 1962. Mimeographed.

[3] For a full description of the procedures used in the development of this classification system, see Dailey, John T., "A System for Classifying Public High Schools." Paper presented at the annual meeting of the American Educational Research Association, Atlantic City, N. J., February, 1962. Mimeographed.

[4] Dailey, John T., "A Survey of the Use of Tests in Public High Schools," p. 5.

[5] Gipe, Melvin W., and Thomas A. Shell, "A Study of Standardized Group Testing Programs in California Public Schools," *California Schools*, vol. 32, June, 1961.

FIGURE 1. THE USE OF VARIOUS STANDARDIZED TESTS, BY TYPE OF HIGH SCHOOL[a]

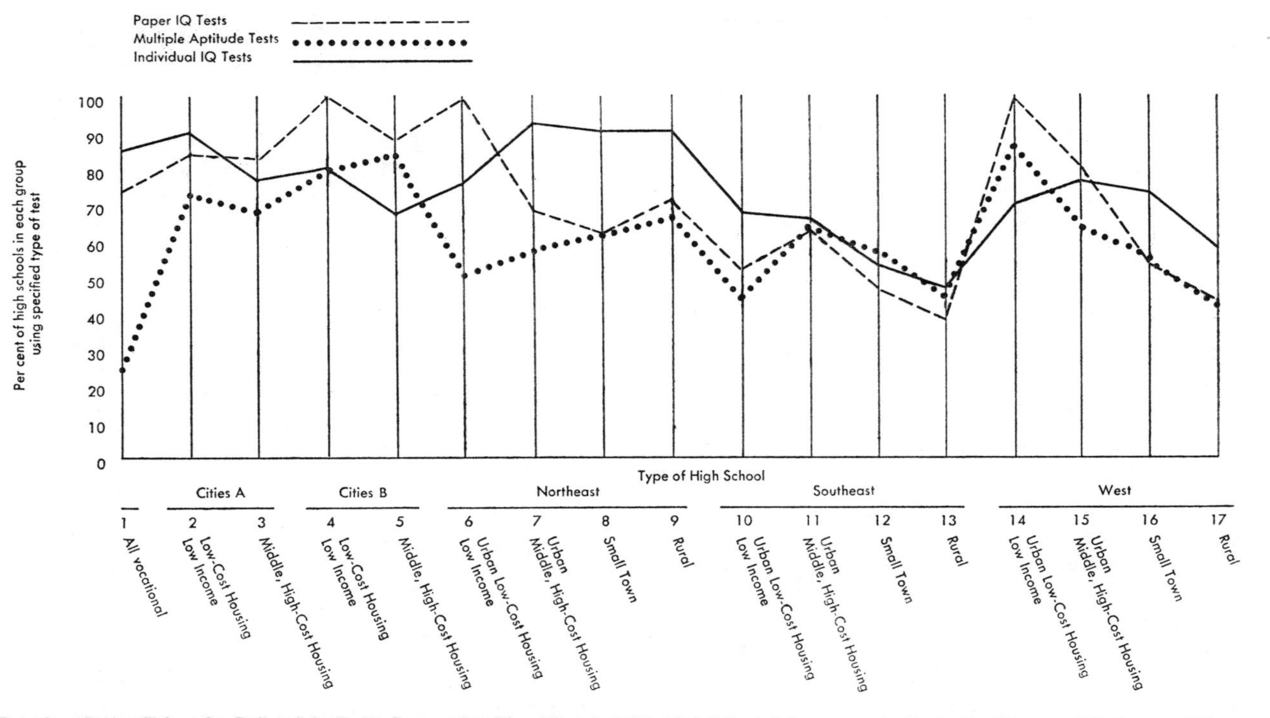

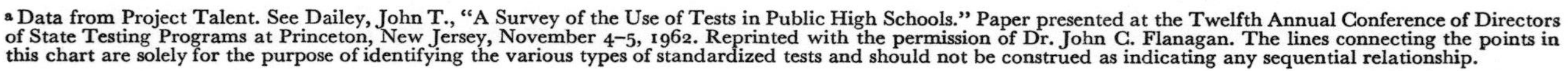
[a] Data from Project Talent. See Dailey, John T., "A Survey of the Use of Tests in Public High Schools." Paper presented at the Twelfth Annual Conference of Directors of State Testing Programs at Princeton, New Jersey, November 4–5, 1962. Reprinted with the permission of Dr. John C. Flanagan. The lines connecting the points in this chart are solely for the purpose of identifying the various types of standardized tests and should not be construed as indicating any sequential relationship.

TABLE 2. A TAXONOMY OF PUBLIC SENIOR HIGH SCHOOLS[a]

Group	Description[b]	Number of Schools
1	All vocational high schools	32
2	Cities A—low-cost housing, low income	27
3	Cities A—middle and high-cost housing	53
4	Cities B—low-cost housing, low income	6
5	Cities B—middle and high-cost housing	21
6	Northeast—urban, low-cost housing and low income	4
7	Northeast—urban, middle and high-cost housing	47
8	Northeast—small-town	31
9	Northeast—rural	21
10	Southeast—urban, low-cost housing and low income	24
11	Southeast—urban, middle and high-cost housing	44
12	Southeast—small-town	40
13	Southeast—rural	98
14	West—urban, low-cost housing and low income	12
15	West—urban, middle and high-cost housing	81
16	West—small-town	135
17	West—rural	131
	Total	807

[a] Data from Project Talent. Reprinted with the permission of Dr. John C. Flanagan.

[b] City sizes:

Cities A—more than 1,500,000 population (1960 census)
Cities B—between 250,000 and 1,499,999 population
Urban—between 5,000 and 249,999 population
Small town—under 5,000 population

that *all* of the 1,642 school districts operating elementary schools or high schools in the state had standardized group testing programs. The selection of tests and the decision as to when and how they were to be used were left to the local district or in many cases to the county superintendent of schools.[1] The result of this

[1] Approximately 1,100 of the 1,686 school districts (including 14 districts not maintaining schools in 1959–1960 and 30 junior college districts) in California were under the jurisdiction of offices of county superintendents of schools, and were provided by them with direct services in the areas of supervision of instruction and pupil personnel services—the areas where standardized testing is an important adjunct. Of the 58 counties, five were constituted as single school districts and the district testing program in each instance was countywide. An additional ten counties, had, through common agreement of the school districts, minimum countywide testing programs. These programs were most common for the elementary school districts.

According to the report, in some counties, each school district under the jurisdiction of the office of the county superintendent of schools was encouraged to select the

local autonomy was considerable variation in the tests used at the various levels. The survey showed that approximately 15 different tests of mental ability were being used throughout the state, 5 different reading readiness tests, 15 different reading achievement tests, 10 different mathematics achievement tests, 10 different English tests, 5 different general science tests, 5 social studies tests, 5 tests of work-study skills, 3 different vocational interest inventories, and 4 multiple aptitude batteries. The predominant testing pattern in grades one through eight was found to include: (1) reading achievement tests given five times from grades three through eight, (2) measures of mathematics achievement in four of the five years represented by grades four through eight, with two testings occurring at grade eight, and (3) tests of English achievement in four of the five years represented by grades four through eight. Scholastic aptitude, vocational interest, and additional achievement tests in other areas were typically given during grades nine through twelve.

In order to create some regularity among the diverse testing programs manifested by the schools in California, the state legislature in 1961 enacted a bill requiring every public school in the state to administer standardized tests of intelligence, reading, arithmetic, and language usage to all pupils in the fifth, eighth, and eleventh grades each year. The dates for test administration are specified in the act. This program went into effect in October, 1962, and it involves approximately 700,000 pupils annually (four different tests apiece) or 2,100,000 different pupils over a three-year period. Since local school districts are still permitted some freedom in the selection of the instruments to be used (for example, they have a choice of six different intelligence tests at grade eight), the development of statewide norms which is an additional goal of the program, is likely to be difficult to attain.

The California program was conceived as a minimum outline and districts are encouraged to supplement it with additional

---

tests to be used and to utilize the test publishers' scoring and statistical analysis services. In the counties operating coordinated programs, the offices of the county superintendents of schools provided the tests, arranged for the scoring, and prepared the statistical analysis of the results. The offices of county superintendents of schools were staffed with personnel to provide consultant service in the area of instruction and pupil personnel matters.

tests. It should also be noted that the State Department of Education in California does not intend to purchase, administer, or score any of the tests, nor will any additional funds be made available to local school districts for this purpose. The local district must finance and administer this program independently. California is notable in that this is the first mandatory statewide testing program designed on this scale (with the possible exception of New York), and it may be the forerunner of similar requirements in other states.

Schools administer both aptitude and achievement tests at all levels, although there is a tendency to make greater use of tests labeled "intelligence tests" in elementary schools, while in junior and senior high schools, tests of the same type are called "scholastic aptitude" tests.[1] Achievement tests are used throughout the grades but probably are given most frequently between grades 4 and 9. As has already been pointed out, tests are produced by many different organizations, but most schools use tests published by commercial or nonprofit agencies that specialize in educational testing (for example, Science Research Associates, Inc., Harcourt, Brace and World, Inc., California Test Bureau, Educational Testing Service). Despite the influence of the financial assistance to secondary schools for testing programs made available under Title V-A of the National Defense Education Act of 1958,[2] elementary schools still appear to be the major users of standardized tests for internal purposes. This may be because it is at this level that teachers begin to discover the abilities of pupils, and the diagnosis of individual strengths and weaknesses is of greatest importance.

Main Objectives and Actual Uses of Tests

The main objectives of internal testing programs in elementary and secondary schools can be summarized as follows:

[1] For a discussion of the distinctions between aptitude, intelligence, and achievement tests, see Chapter VI.

[2] For a summary of the act, see U.S. Department of Health, Education, and Welfare, Office of Education, *Report on the National Defense Education Act*, Fiscal Year Ending June 30, 1960, Government Printing Office, Washington, 1961; or U.S. Senate, Committee on Labor and Public Welfare, *The National Defense Education Act of 1958:* A Summary and Analysis of the Act, Government Printing Office, Washington, 1958. The influence of this act on secondary school testing will be discussed below.

1. To promote better adjustment, motivation, and progress of the individual student through a better understanding of his abilities and weaknesses, both on his own part and on the part of his teachers and parents;
2. To aid in decisions about the readiness of the pupil for exposure to new subject matter;
3. To measure the progress of pupils;
4. To aid in the grade placement of individuals and the special grouping of children for instructional purposes within classes or grades;
5. To aid in the identification of children with special problems or abilities;
6. To provide objective measures of the relative effectiveness of alternative teaching techniques, curriculum content, and the like;
7. To aid in the identification of special needs from the standpoint of the efficiency of the school relative to other schools.

While most school administrators would subscribe to this list of objectives, it is difficult to judge the degree to which a given school actually makes maximum use of the tests it administers. Table 3 presents replies to a question on test use which was asked in the survey of testing practices in Michigan conducted by Frank Womer.

In addition to a survey of the extent of testing in American public high schools, Project Talent investigators also asked about the way tests were used by the schools in their sample. Figure 2 shows how schools in each of the 17 taxonomy groups[1] responded to five questions concerned with test usage. Regional, class, and rural-urban differences are apparent on most of the items. While these items by no means exhaust the possible uses of standardized tests, this study also is indicative of the diversity of testing practice.

While the results of the studies reported above are self-explanatory, two observations can be made. First, reported use of test scores and actual use may differ considerably. Within a school system a particular school, teacher, or counselor might not use test results in the manner specified by the superintendent for the system as a whole. The most frequently mentioned use of test

[1] See p. 64.

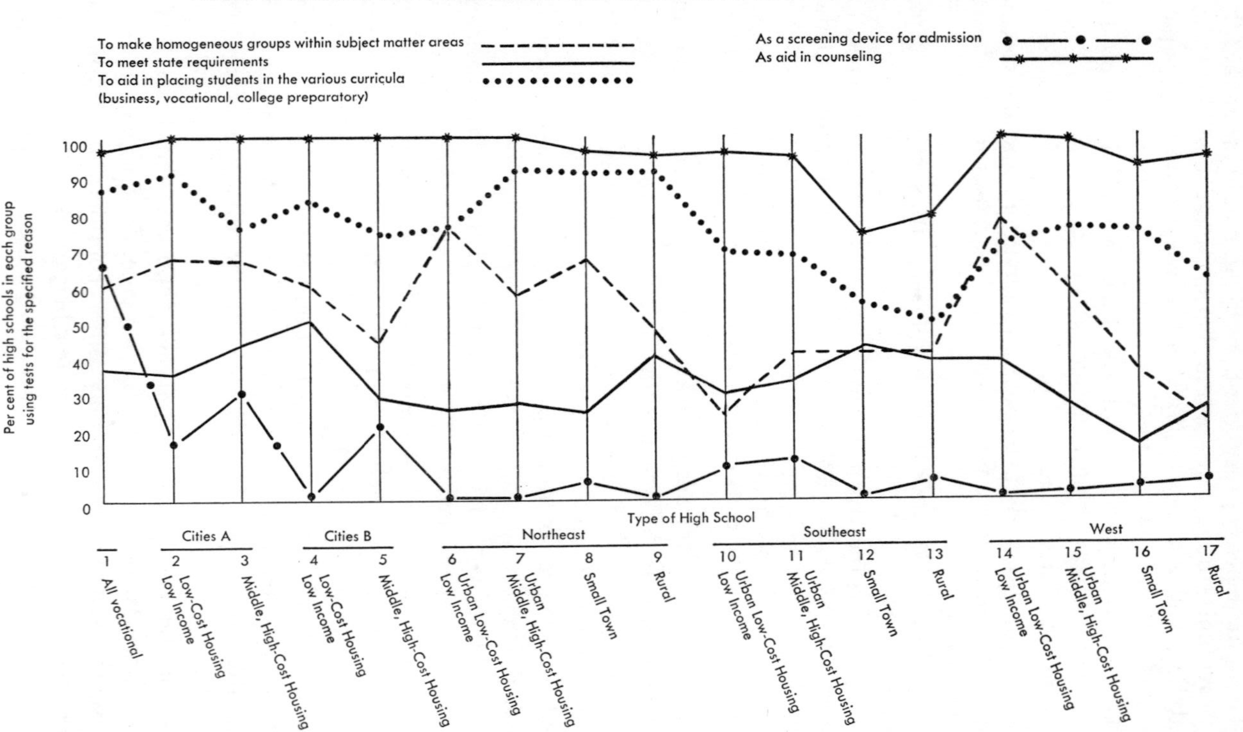

FIGURE 2. REASONS FOR STANDARDIZED TESTING IN DIFFERENT TYPES OF HIGH SCHOOLS[a]

[a] Data from Project Talent. See Dailey, John T., *op. cit.* Reprinted with the permission of Dr. John C. Flanagan. The lines connecting the points in this chart are solely for the purpose of identifying the various uses of standardized tests and should not be construed as indicating any sequential relationship.

TABLE 3. REPLIES TO A QUESTION ON TEST USE IN A MICHIGAN SURVEY

Use(s) of test results	Percentage of school systems reporting using test results in various ways				
	Size of school systems[a]				Percentage of all systems
	A	B	C	D	
Development of pupil self-knowledge	73	78	59	52	68
Teacher diagnosis of pupil strengths and weaknesses	98	95	93	87	94
Evaluation of curriculum	71	60	53	74	61
Development of educational and vocational goals	68	73	58	57	65
Teacher analysis of class achievement	71	61	69	48	64
Placement in particular classes	83	78	58	43	68
Identification of the exceptional child	88	77	76	57	76
Determination of reasonable levels of achievement	71	74	61	52	67
Evaluation of educational research	34	11	16	9	16
Development of parental understanding of pupil	68	68	68	57	67
Motivation for increased learning	66	62	42	35	47
Improvement of public relations	44	35	36	30	36
Development of continuous program of teacher in-service education	37	31	29	22	30

[a] This classification corresponds to the generally used athletic classification of schools, with Class A being the largest and Class D the smallest.

results according to the Womer survey is teacher diagnosis of pupil strengths and weaknesses. Yet this is almost entirely dependent on the interest, motivation, and qualifications of the individual teacher, and we would expect considerable variation from teacher to teacher even in school systems where teachers received explicit instructions as to the way scores are to be used. Hastings has shown that teachers themselves are frequently unaware of the amount of reliance they place on test scores in making decisions about a student.[1]

While the discrepancy between reported and actual use of scores probably tends to overestimate their usage owing to the prestige attached to testing and a desire on the part of administrators to justify increased expenditures on testing, the evidence is that some teachers, counselors, and principals rely more heavily

[1] Hastings, J. Thomas, and others, *The Use of Test Results*. Bureau of Educational Research, Urbana, Ill., 1960.

on test results than they realize. All of this would indicate that evaluations of test usage are generally unreliable. It is significant that, despite a "comfortable optimism" about guidance activities on the part of administrators in schools having extensive testing programs, Hastings found no differences in Illinois between such schools and schools having less extensive programs with respect to how much knowledge children felt their teachers had about them. Nor were any differences found in the amount of information children had about vocations in the two kinds of school systems.

The second observation concerns the fact that the percentage of school systems reporting a given usage of results is surprisingly low in several categories. For example, only a little more than half of the Class D schools report they use tests to identify the gifted child, and Womer points out that from a fourth to a third of the Class A and Class B schools do not use test scores to improve pupil self-knowledge or parental understanding of pupils, or to develop educational and vocational goals. As Womer puts it, "One can't help wondering what the counselors in these systems do."[1]

It is clear that our knowledge about the way test results are being used by schools is limited. We do know that schools report a wide variety of uses and that if one considers the percentages of school systems reporting all the different uses of test results, one finds that there is a relationship between size of the school and number of uses reported. We do not know much about the relationship between reported and actual test use or why some schools that have testing programs do not report that they use test scores for the most obvious and potentially useful purposes. The importance of information about how tests are being used makes this a fruitful area for research.

School Personnel Involved in Test Administration and Interpretation

A consideration of the individuals who are responsible for the administration of internal testing programs may shed some light

[1] Womer, Frank B., *op. cit.*, p. 52.

on the problem of how test scores are used. Since test interpretation and consequently optimum usage requires training in measurement techniques, only those schools that can afford to hire counselors and administrators with some experience in testing are in a position to make the most of test data in evaluating either students or curricula. However, the schools that do the most testing and are therefore in greatest need of trained counselors and measurement specialists are the elementary schools. And this is the level at which funds for specialists have been least available. We have pointed out that upwards of 80 per cent of all elementary schools in the United States are presently using standardized tests one or more times between the first and sixth grades. It is probable that the bulk of these schools do not have a testing specialist on their staff. Inevitably, the chances for misinterpretation or merely wastage of test results are thereby increased.

The survey of testing programs in Michigan schools supports the view that classroom teachers bear the primary responsibility for the administration and scoring of tests and the recording of scores at the elementary level.[1] In addition to the administration of tests, it was found that elementary classroom teachers are primarily responsible in Michigan for the interpretation of intelligence test scores to pupils and they share with administrators (mainly the principal) the responsibility of interpreting scores to parents.[2] In the case of achievement-test results, classroom teachers tend to bear primary responsibility for interpretation of scores to both parents and pupils, according to the Michigan study. Elementary teachers, on the whole, have had little or no training in psychometrics and it is probably not practical at the present time to expect such qualifications. In addition, it has been argued[3] that the primary task of the classroom teacher is to teach and it is unjust to expect her to perform, in addition, the roles of psychological diagnostician and therapist. It appears, therefore, that the elementary teacher frequently is being placed in a posi-

[1] *Ibid.*, pp. 27–32.

[2] Just what is involved in "the interpretation of test scores" is not clear from the data. Presumably schools vary with respect to methods of test interpretation.

[3] See, for example, Sarason, Seymour B., and others, *Anxiety in Elementary School Children*, John Wiley and Sons, New York, 1960.

tion for which she is not qualified, and one which may distract her from her primary function, that of teaching.[1]

We have already noted that schools differ considerably in their testing practices according to their size, with the larger systems doing more testing. The larger school system, as might be expected, is also more likely to employ a testing specialist with responsibility for the development of a systemwide test program. In the smaller system, on the other hand, the principal or the superintendent of schools is likely to have responsibility for the testing activities, and we are again faced with a shortage of people who are qualified to administer and interpret standardized tests.

It is hard to evaluate the impact of this problem. While experts are in agreement that it is a good thing to know something about testing before one attempts to use standardized tests, there are very few systematic data available on the effects of ignorance about testing procedures and principles on the way tests are administered or the way results are interpreted. There is some evidence which suggests that in cases where the test giver has little knowledge about what tests measure, test scores tend either to be used in overly formalized ways (for example, the establishment of rigid cutting points for admission to special classes and the like) or else neglected in favor of other sources of information about pupils. Hastings[2] found that, contrary to popular belief, secondary school teachers who had had training in psychometrics tended to place more importance on the value of test scores in making decisions about students. However, he also found that psychometric training led to a somewhat more moderate attitude toward test scores as opposed to an extreme belief (either negative or positive) about their value. These findings may not hold at the elementary school level, but they indicate that we need to know more about teachers' attitudes toward tests and test results, particularly if they are the ones who are responsible for most of the actual test administration and interpretation.

[1] In addition to considerations of the adequacy of the teacher to interpret test scores, Sarason (*op. cit.*) has presented data which indicate that the teacher may have an important effect on generating attitudes toward learning, tests, failure, and success, which in turn affect the level of anxiety with which children approach a test. The effect of this anxiety on test scores themselves will be discussed in Chapter VI.

[2] Hastings, J. Thomas, and others, *op. cit.*

Psychometric Training for School Personnel

There are two sources of encouragement for those who may be worried about the lack of psychometric training of teachers and administrators. The first is that there are many places where a teacher can turn for help in understanding the intricacies of standardized tests. We have already mentioned that most test publishers maintain a staff of salesmen to assist educators in selecting the most appropriate tests and, in many cases, in interpreting the results. Also, the literature on testing practices and pitfalls is voluminous and informative. In addition, many state universities and state departments of education maintain advisory services for the assistance of local school systems and individuals who are involved in standardized testing. Data on state testing programs and services were collected in 1958 by the Educational Testing Service.[1] Replies received from 30 states and 2 territorial departments of education and from 23 state colleges and universities described 31 statewide testing programs in 17 states and two territories. Consultant and advisory services available to schools were reported by 28 of the 32 state agencies and 22 of the 23 colleges and universities. Many of these organizations also supply tests (loan, rental, or sale) and most sponsor workshops for counselors and other school officials in order to increase knowledge of testing procedures.

Another attack on the problem of training school personnel in testing techniques has been made by the Counseling and Guidance Institutes Section of the U.S. Office of Education. This office is charged with the administration of a training program for school guidance counselors under the National Defense Education Act of 1958. Since that year the government has been financing the operation of Guidance Institutes on the campuses of leading colleges, at which currently over 600 school counselors annually are engaged in a year's study to improve their knowledge of counseling methods, including measurement techniques. In addition, a large number of summer guidance counselor training schools have been established under the National Defense Education Act, with the result that since 1958 the counselor-

[1] Educational Testing Service, *Large-Scale Programs of Testing for Guidance.* Princeton, N. J., March, 1958, pp. 35–43.

student ratio in secondary schools has improved from 750/1 to 350/1. Thus far, the primary impact of this program has been on secondary schools, but it is clear that increasing the number of trained counselors will have a direct effect on the use of standardized tests in elementary schools. In general, it probably can be concluded that misuse of standardized tests has not resulted from negligence on the part of professionals in the field but simply from a lack of trained manpower relative to the number of people who have been forced by circumstances into the role of tester.

The Cost of Internal Testing

The expense of commercially distributed tests is relatively low when one considers the amount of work that goes into the preparation of a standardized test instrument. According to the figures received from the major test publishers by the American Textbook Publishers Institute and reported in its annual survey, the average price of a single test in 1960 was about 11.5 cents and the range of company average prices was from 2.6 cents to 20 cents a test. Answer sheets averaged 4.52 cents apiece, with company averages here ranging from 2.4 to 11 cents a sheet. While the per pupil expenditure is considerably more than 10 cents a year because of scoring costs and the fact that the student may take several tests, the total cost on the average does not appear to be exorbitant. In Keck's study of testing and evaluation practices in New England,[1] the median annual expenditure for pupil appraisal programs including materials and scoring services, was 40 cents per student. This figure corresponds almost exactly to the reported median annual expenditure in Michigan schools,[2] and while it does not take into account schools that spend considerably more or less, it is indicative of the moderate cost of standardized testing as a means of gathering information about pupils. It is also interesting to note that Womer found only minor differences between schools falling into different size categories with respect to expenditures on testing in Michigan, with the Class A schools having a lower median expenditure (35 cents) than the Class B (40 cents), the Class C (43 cents), or the Class D

[1] Keck, Winston, *op. cit.*

[2] Womer, Frank B., *op. cit.*

(40 cents) schools. It should be remembered, however, that salaries of persons engaged in testing are not included in these figures, and it is in this area that the larger systems are spending considerably more than the smaller systems.

Federal Aid for Secondary School Testing

Internal and external testing in secondary schools was given a tremendous boost in 1958 as a result of Title V-A of the National Defense Education Act, which made funds available to states to "establish and maintain a program for testing aptitudes and abilities of students in public secondary schools, and, if authorized by law, in other secondary schools, to identify students with outstanding aptitudes and abilities, reports of which may be used for the following purposes: (a) to provide such information about the aptitudes and abilities of secondary school students as may be needed by secondary school guidance personnel in carrying out their duties; and (b) to provide information to other educational institutions relative to the educational potential of students seeking admission to such institutions."[1] Specifically excluded from federal financial participation under Title V-A are all personality tests, personal or social adjustment tests, and projective techniques. "Testing" as defined in Section 504 (a) of the Act means "the use of tests which measure abilities from which aptitudes for the individual's educational development validly may be inferred."[2]

Federal assistance is also extended to private secondary schools under Section 504 (b) of Title V-A, in which occurs the statement that all children attending nonpublic secondary schools should have the opportunity to be tested sometime during their secondary school attendance in order that the test results may be used in identifying students with outstanding ability. Under the NDEA, schools have considerable freedom to select whatever tests they wish within the limits of the act, and the latest figures indicate that approximately 35 per cent of all the testing going on in

[1] U.S. Department of Health, Education, and Welfare, Office of Education, "Guidance, Counseling, and Testing: Identification and Encouragement of Able Students—State Programs." Regulations, Sections 501 through 504(a) of Title V, Part A, National Defense Education Act of 1958, pp. 7–8.

[2] *Ibid.*, p. 8.

secondary schools is being financed by the federal government. It is not clear whether this figure includes an estimate of external testing. By June 30, 1960, all 50 states, the District of Columbia, Puerto Rico, Guam, and the Virgin Islands were participating in the testing program. During the fiscal year 1960, $13.4 million was paid to states (on a matching basis, by state and/or local funds) for guidance counseling and testing programs.[1]

Internal Testing by Private Schools

Thus far we have neglected to say anything specific about internal testing programs in private elementary and secondary schools. The objectives and problems faced by private schools are much the same as those encountered by public schools but the financial resources and professional skills for a large scale testing program are often harder to find. Owing to their smaller size, private schools, in addition, typically have relied more on personal appraisal and individual attention for all students rather than for a chosen few. On the other hand, individual intelligence tests may be given for diagnostic purposes more frequently than in the public school. This is particularly true at the elementary level where private schools are freer to experiment with alternative methods of grading and pupil evaluation than public institutions.

Private schools, however, have their own testing agency, the Educational Records Bureau, which is a nonprofit organization much like Educational Testing Service. The Educational Records Bureau provides a variety of testing, scoring, and record-keeping services for some 750 member independent schools (plus 100 public schools), including both elementary and secondary schools. In 1960–1961 member schools gave approximately 350,000 achievement and aptitude tests in two administrations (fall and spring), of which more than half were scored by the Educational Records Bureau and the results returned to the participating schools, along with the interpretive norms indicating the position of the school relative to other similar schools in terms of pupil performance. The Educational Records Bureau

[1] U.S. Department of Health, Education, and Welfare, Office of Education, *Report on the National Defense Education Act*, p. 17.

makes use of commercially published tests, such as the Kuhlman-Anderson Intelligence Test and the Stanford Achievement Test, but leaves the decision as to particular test and even the extent of participation in the fall and spring programs entirely to the school. While any one of the schools could order tests directly from the publisher, the Educational Records Bureau feels that one of the chief benefits of its service is the provision of norms to member and participating schools so that the school can interpret scores and compare the performance of its students with that of students from similar schools, thus leading to curriculum evaluation, improved guidance, and the like.

Internal Testing at the College and University Level

Testing for admission to undergraduate and graduate institutions will be discussed below under the heading of external testing. However, standardized tests are used internally by colleges and universities for two main purposes: (1) for evaluating both individually and collectively the abilities of incoming students in order to make decisions about programs of study, assignment of advanced standing, and the like; and (2) in order to provide evidence of the general level of abilities of the undergraduate body as a part of the process of making application for accreditation and similar kinds of professional recognition from the academic community. Testing in order to evaluate incoming students, of course, is done primarily by institutions that do not require test scores as part of the information used in the admissions process. In such instances, information about the abilities of students in the freshman class is important in enabling advisers to help students choose the most appropriate program of study and to identify individuals who might encounter difficulties.

The second kind of testing is done by smaller nonaccredited colleges that wish to indicate their concern for the quality of their educational program and to demonstrate that their students are comparable in ability to those in accredited institutions.

Most internal standardized testing at the college level is restricted to the freshman year, probably because colleges, except for the nonaccredited institutions, are usually not under any pressure to keep up with other schools in terms of the number of services provided for students outside of the purely academic course material. Colleges are typically not evaluated on the strength of their guidance program, and the result is that colleges tend to test only when it is necessary in order to get specific information about students for a specific purpose, for example, in evaluating an application for advanced placement.

Two Testing Programs

In order to provide a somewhat more coherent view of internal testing in public elementary and secondary schools, two samples will be provided in the following paragraphs. The first is a description of a "typical" testing program in "Michiganville," a fictional Michigan school. The second example is a somewhat simplified outline of the actual testing program that is prescribed by the Bureau of Educational Research of the Board of Education of New York for all public schools in the city. These examples are not claimed to be representative of testing programs throughout the country, nor are they presented as ideal programs toward which school systems should be working. Instead, they are offered solely for the purpose of indicating the extent to which children in some schools are being exposed to standardized tests.

"Michiganville." The Michigan example is taken from Womer's survey of testing practices in that state, which has been referred to above. Womer is careful to point out that "Michiganville" is probably not exactly like any actual school system in the state. It should be noted also that since small schools were underrepresented in the Michigan survey results, the following "typical" testing program is more likely to be typical of a medium to large school system and one that is above average in resources.

> Michiganville's testing program consists of a readiness test at kindergarten, reading (achievement) tests at grades 2 and 3, intelligence tests at grades 3, 5, 7, and 9, achievement batteries at grades 4, 6, 8, and 12, interest inventories at grades 9 and 12, an aptitude battery at grade 10, and an algebra aptitude test at grade 8.
>
> In the elementary grades, the teachers administer, score the tests, and record the scores. In the secondary grades, teachers administer the achievement tests and interest inventories, while the counselor

> administers the other tests. At the secondary level, the counselor does part of the scoring while part of it is done by an outside agency, and the scores are recorded by the counselor or by a clerk.
>
> The interpretation of test results in the Michiganville elementary schools is handled by classroom teachers and principals, the teachers having responsibility for interpreting achievement test results while the principal becomes involved more often with interpreting intelligence test results. At the secondary level the counselor is most apt to handle test interpretation, no matter what the test area may be.
>
> The Michiganville schools use individual pupil conferences and individual parent conferences for reporting test results to pupils and parents. In addition, summary statistics of test results are prepared for the use of teachers and administrators.
>
> Test results are used for teacher diagnosis of pupil and class strengths and weaknesses, for determining reasonable levels of achievement, for developing pupil self-knowledge, for developing parental understanding of pupils, for developing educational and vocational goals, for identifying the exceptional child, for the placing of pupils, and for evaluating the curriculum. The Michiganville schools spend about $.40 per year per pupil for tests and other testing materials (not including counselors' salaries).[1]

It should be noted that there are only two grades between kindergarten and the final year of high school in which standardized tests are not administered, grade 1 and grade 11 (when many students would be taking externally administered tests for college entrance and scholarship awards). In four grades, 3, 8, 9, and 12, students take more than one kind of test. We also note that test interpretation and administration at the elementary level are likely to be handled by teachers, or in some cases by the principal, and that it is at this level that intelligence tests (which may become difficult to interpret) are typically given. While it is claimed that individual pupil and parent conferences are used to report scores made on tests, interpreting this statement to mean that all scores are reported to all children and all or most parents in this manner is unrealistic, when one considers the number of tests being administered.

New York City. The testing program in New York City public schools provides something of a contrast with the program just described, but a great many basic similarities can be discerned.

[1] Womer, Frank B., *op. cit.*, p. 55.

For a variety of reasons, testing in New York City schools is more extensive than in the Michigan example. The heterogeneity of the students and the many problems faced by administrators and teachers in attempting to provide for the educational needs that result from this diversity of student backgrounds are important factors in the extent of the testing program. The New York school system is also unique because of its enormous size, each elementary grade level having approximately 80,000 enrolled students.[1] The advantages, as well as the disadvantages of the resulting bureaucratic organization, are reflected in the testing activities carried on in the local schools.

The decision to administer a standardized test to a pupil or class in a New York City school can come from any one of four different sources. A minimum citywide testing program is established by the Bureau of Educational Research, which also acts as an advisory agency for all testing activities. Additional testing may also be done in selected areas by Bureau personnel for research purposes. Second, the superintendent in charge of the elementary, junior high, or high school division may decide to administer additional tests to pupils in schools in that division. Third, any Assistant Superintendent of Schools with responsibility for a particular district of the city may approve testing in the schools in his district. And finally, any school principal or guidance person in the school (with the approval of the principal) is permitted to select a test from the list of approved tests circulated by the Bureau of Educational Research and give it to students in that school or in a specific class within the school. In practice, district superintendents of schools, and occasionally an entire division, will institute additional testing on a group basis, but the extra testing (that is, in addition to citywide programs) done by guidance personnel is primarily for special purposes (for example, to check an individual's performance on a citywide test) and is frequently carried out on an individual basis.

The citywide testing program is similar to that used in other large city school systems, especially Los Angeles, Chicago,

[1] In 1960–1961, 460,738 pupils were promoted in the first six grades. This is a rate of 96.2 per cent of the total enrollment. In the same year, 181,391 students were promoted in the three junior high school grades (7, 8, 9).

Detroit, Baltimore, Cincinnati, and Cleveland.[1] Test results are used for administrative purposes by superintendents and principals, for instructional purposes by supervisors and teachers, and for guidance purposes by counselors. The Bureau of Educational Research, in addition to supervising the citywide testing program, conducts research in an effort to improve its selection of tests used in the program, holds teacher-training conferences on testing, and reviews all commercially available tests that are submitted for listing by the Board of Education. It has also constructed and published six standardized tests that are specifically designed to fit the curriculum requirements of the New York City system.

The core of the citywide testing program is the administration of both intelligence and achievement tests in grades 1, 3, 6, and 8. The Bureau of Educational Research is responsible for this testing both from a logistic standpoint and from the technical standpoint of test selection, assistance to school administrators, and the like. In addition, the Bureau provides scoring services for the intelligence tests given in grade 8, and compiles citywide statistical analyses of scores on all tests administered in grades 3, 6, and 8. In grade 1[2] the achievement test administered is a reading readiness test which is administered at the discretion of the teacher when the class has reached the appropriate level. The intelligence test administered at this level is the Pintner-Cunningham Primary Test which yields an IQ estimate. The results of both these tests are used only by the school.

All of the succeeding citywide surveys, on which norms are computed for the city as a whole (grades 3, 6, and 8), consist of an intelligence test (Otis Quick in grades 3 and 6, Pintner General Ability Test in grade 8), and achievement tests in reading (Metropolitan Achievement Series) and arithmetic (New York Inventory of Mathematical Concepts, Metropolitan Achievement Series, and New York City Arithmetic Computations Test). In addition to the surveys conducted by the Bureau

[1] Bureau of Educational Research, Special Memorandum No. 100-4-10-61, Re: *Appraisal of the City-Wide Testing Programs.* Board of Education, New York City, 1961, p. 1.

[2] Some schools give an IQ test at the kindergarten level. This, however, is at the discretion of the school.

of Educational Research, the Junior High School Division regularly administers a reading achievement test in grade 7 and (in cooperation with the Senior High School Division) administers the Iowa Tests of Educational Development (an achievement battery) to pupils in grade 9 and new entrants in grade 10. Although New York students take a reading achievement test in grade 6 (and their scores are reported to the junior high school which they are entering), they are tested again in the middle of the seventh grade, the practice being to report scores on the latter tests to parents on their midyear report cards.[1]

The tests we have mentioned, however, do not by any means exhaust the testing activities of New York schools. These tests were supplemented in 1960–1961 by reading and arithmetic tests at grade 2, arithmetic achievement tests at grades 4 and 5, another reading achievement measure at grade 9, and any additional tests given by particular counselors or principals in specific schools. New York City public school students therefore take a minimum of 19 different tests (including one achievement battery) between grades 1 and 9, including at least one test every year. Internal testing is rare after the ninth grade (or the tenth for incoming students), but a variety of different external tests, including the New York State Regents' examinations, the College Board tests, and the various state and national scholarship examinations are given instead. A pupil may also take entrance tests in the ninth grade for admission to one of New York's special high schools if he is an outstanding student or has special talents in such areas as music, art, or fashion and design.

While test results are used for the same purposes in New York schools as in most other schools (for administration, instruction, and guidance), the size of the system has made it necessary for administrators to specify the use of scores in making certain critical decisions about the pupil. These decisions concern promotion, placement of the child in special sections for gifted students, classification of retarded children for placement in

[1] One of the advantages of this practice which, incidentally, is not confined to the New York public school system, is that it resolves the grading dilemma created by the student of below average intelligence who is working up to the limit of his ability, but still doing poor work. In New York public schools this student may earn an "A" for his effort in the seventh grade, but his reading achievement test score is reported along with his mark to show the level of his reading achievement.

special classes, and decisions about the courses open to a particular student (for example, algebra vs. home economics). These uses of test scores are illustrated by the instructions issued in September, 1960, for the selection of children for IG ("intellectually gifted") classes.

IG grouping is typically accomplished in the third grade on the basis of citywide survey test scores.[1] A minimum Stanford-Binet IQ of 125 is generally required for admittance to the program. However, since it is not practical to give individual intelligence tests to 80,000 children in the third grade, a formula is used which takes into account both the child's score on the Otis Quick intelligence test and his scores on the third grade reading and arithmetic achievement tests. According to the formula, a minimum grade score of 4.8 on the Metropolitan Achievement Primary Reading Test given in the third grade and a minimum score of the 60th percentile on the N. Y. Inventory of Mathematical Concepts for grade 2 are required for IG grouping. Under some circumstances a score on the Otis test indicating an IQ lower than 125 is acceptable if the corresponding achievement test scores are above the minimum level.

However, a child possessing the minimum IQ of 125 might not be admitted to IG classes if his achievement scores were below the minimum requirement. The following statement appears in the directive on IG selection.

> Since the IGC program requires a high degree of verbal ability, skill in this area is one important criterion for the placement of children. As a result, there may occasionally be individuals who will not be eligible for admission to IG classes because of reading deficiencies, although they possess the minimum IQ of 125. Children with such deficiencies would have serious difficulties in functioning in IG classes and might best be placed in other appropriate classes in the grade.[2]

In general, although school officials indicate that every effort is made to re-test children who present unusual problems and to

[1] Some schools do not have IG classes, in which case they are required to give a qualified child an "enriched" program and are allotted additional funds for this purpose.

[2] Bureau of Educational Research, "Instructions for the Selection of Children for IG Classes for September, 1960," p. 1. Mimeographed.

provide for the needs of children who may be deprived because of their cultural background, it is likely that the size of the school system and the number of decisions that have to be made each year tend to produce a degree of inflexibility in the use of test results. This rigidity may contribute to a lessening of opportunities for mobility on the part of culturally deprived individuals that, in the long run, may be dysfunctional for the system as a whole. The solution, however, is not necessarily the abandonment of standardized testing but rather an accentuated vigilance on maintaining flexibility in the interpretation of test scores. The fact that a decision made in grade three may have far-reaching effects on the child and that tests may, as a result, have the characteristics of a self-fulfilling prophecy cannot be overemphasized. This point will be discussed in some detail in Chapter VII.

EXTERNAL TESTING

What do we mean by external testing? What kinds of tests are included under our definition of external testing? How are test results used and what changes can we expect in the future uses of external test program scores? What is the rationale of external testing and why do we have so many different testing programs? What effects do external testing programs have on schools, children, and parents?

As defined, external testing may take place either within a particular school or in some other place, but it is designed primarily to benefit some organization other than the school that the children attend.

Externally administered tests fall into three main categories: (1) tests used by schools, colleges, and other organizations for making decisions about admissions and scholarship awards, (2) tests given by state or local governmental agencies for the purpose of setting standards and evaluating schools, and (3) tests given by external research organizations in the process of evaluating teaching methods, comparing schools, or estimating the resources of talent in various parts of the United States. External testing is not, of course, restricted to national or even state programs, although these are the activities that receive the greatest attention. Most private secondary schools and some public schools give entrance examinations to all applicants for admission and while many schools participate in the national Secondary School Admissions Testing, some, like the Bronx High School of Science in New York City, give their own entrance examination.

In addition to the well-known College Board tests and the newer American College Testing program, a partial list of the national testing programs includes the National Merit Scholarship Qualifying Test, the Betty Crocker Scholarship Program, the Naval Reserve Officer Training Corps Scholarship Program, the National Honor Society Testing Program, the National League of Nursing Tests, the National Mathematics Tests, the General Motors Scholarship Program, and the Advanced Placement testing program.[1] We have already mentioned the Secondary School Admissions Testing Program administered by the Educational Testing Service.

At the state level we find a host of external testing programs, with New York winning the distinction of having the largest number of different programs; for example, the New York Regents' examinations, the New York University Selective Admissions Test, the Junior High School Survey Tests, the Le Moyne College Test, the Regents' State Scholarship Tests, the Junior High School Scholastic Ability Tests, the State Employment Test, the Civil Service Tests, the State Labor Department Test, and the Syracuse University Citizenship test. New York is not alone, however. Ohio has seven programs; California, Illinois, and Kansas have five each; Texas and Kentucky, four; Minnesota, three; and so on.

External testing is not entirely confined to the secondary schools, although the bulk of it probably occurs during this period. The college senior who plans to attend graduate or professional school faces another battery of national external admissions tests. The Law School Admissions Test, the Admissions Test for Graduate Study in Business, and the Graduate Record

[1] Hastings, J. Thomas, "Testing Programs Available to Schools" in *Measurement and Research in Today's Schools:* Report of the Twenty-Fifth Educational Conference, Sponsored by the Educational Records Bureau and the American Council on Education. American Council on Education, Washington, 1960. Of course, a distinction must be made between routine college admissions testing and special scholarship competitions.

Examination are all examples of external testing programs at the college level.

It also should be pointed out that not all junior high, high school, or college students take externally sponsored tests. Most tests are aimed at a particular group of students, usually those of high ability. In addition, in most cases even the outstanding student does not have to participate in the testing program if he does not wish to do so. However, if the school, college, professional school, or graduate department to which the individual is applying requires a test score, the student has little choice. More freedom is possible if the student is not in need of scholarship aid, but the financially independent student is becoming increasingly rare as tuition fees rise rapidly throughout the country. A particular school does not have to take part in a national testing program either, but in practice the school must provide its students with all possible opportunities to win scholarships and gain admission to colleges if it is to live up to its responsibilities to students, as well as maintain its reputation.

Goals of External Testing

The main purpose of scholarship and admissions tests is, of course, to identify those individuals who are likely to benefit most from a college education or other specialized training in order to make maximum use of our educational facilities. The traditional criterion for measuring how much a student has "benefited" from an educational experience has been his average grade.[1] Consequently, admissions and scholarship tests have been evaluated principally on their ability to predict a student's grade average in college or professional school (or high school in the case of secondary school admissions).

Studies have shown, however, that just as good a predictor of college success is the applicant's high school record.[2] Why not

[1] The efficacy of this assumption will be discussed in more detail in Chapter VI. While there is little doubt that intelligence, college performance, and success are all related, it may turn out that we are grossly neglecting additional important factors in the process of "benefiting from a college education," and thereby lowering our ability to predict ultimate success in life, or contribution to society.

[2] See Holland, J. L., *A Program of Research on the Identification, Motivation, and Training of Talented Students*. Technical Report No. 5, National Merit Scholarship Corporation, Evanston, Ill.

then rely solely on reports from the last school attended by the student in the making of decisions about scholarships and admission? The problem faced by the college or graduate school admissions officer is one of evaluating the high school records of applicants who have extremely varied backgrounds and who come from schools with different standards. As the number of applicants to institutions of higher learning has increased, and, in particular, the proportion applying from public schools, it has become more and more important to establish a common standard against which students with different backgrounds can be evaluated. National testing programs have provided this standard. Used in conjunction with high school grades (or college grades), test scores have helped Deans of Admissions to predict success in their institutions.[1]

Another factor in the rapid growth of external testing programs has been the growing international competition for leadership in the world community. This has produced tremendous pressure to make maximum use of all our potential resources of talent. It has meant providing talented individuals, regardless of background, with the opportunity to develop most fully their potential. In turn, this has resulted specifically in an increase in the number of scholarships being offered for outstanding high school students, and generally, in the concern for making sure that no able students are bypassed.[2]

It has frequently been pointed out by psychometricians that, from a practical standpoint, large-scale testing is still the best way

[1] Recent work by Benjamin S. Bloom at the University of Chicago indicates that it may be possible to increase the correlation between high school grades and college grades from the present .50 level to .80 by taking into account the "institutional variation" of the high school. See Bloom, Benjamin S., *The Use of Academic Prediction Scales for Counseling and Selecting College Entrants*, The Free Press of Glencoe, New York, 1961. Attempts to replicate Bloom's work (by Lindquist and others) have not resulted in correlations as high as those reported by Bloom. Further work in this area is clearly indicated before a final judgment as to the relative merits of the two positions can be made.

[2] It has been pointed out that even if we restrict our attention to the extremely bright individuals in the population we are still talking about a sizable number of people. "In the United States there are 180,000 in the top 0.1 per cent of the population. Of these 'one in a thousand,' 84,000 are in the productive age range of 25 to 64 years. Probably 10,000 are in college and close to 40,000 in the elementary and high school grades." Warren, Johnathan R., Review of Adam Yarmolinsky's *Recognition of Excellence* (The Free Press of Glencoe, New York, 1960) in *Harvard Educational Review*, vol. 31, Summer, 1961, p. 339.

of selecting among hundreds of thousands of applicants for scholarships and college admissions. While this view does not preclude the possibility of developing a better technique for identifying the most talented young people in the society, it does place some of the responsibility for such an innovation in the hands of the critics of present testing practices. Actually, most of the organizations that sponsor admissions testing and scholarship granting programs are greatly concerned with the problem of increasing the accuracy and efficiency of their methods. But the task is a formidable one. One of the first national talent searches, that by the National Merit Scholarship Corporation,[1] sifted 586,813 students in 15,095 high schools in 1960–1961 in order to select 1146 Merit Scholars (including 203 Honorary Merit Scholars who received no financial aid). The job of objectively evaluating half a million candidates annually in order to award a thousand scholarships is an enormous one, and it necessitates the use of relatively simple numerical techniques at least in the early stages. Thus, the National Merit Scholarship Qualifying Test (NMSQT) was developed. This test includes proficiency subtests in English, mathematics, social studies reading, natural science reading, and word usage. The initial reduction in the size of the candidate group is made almost entirely on the basis of scores on this test. In most cases, this score must fall above the 98th percentile in order to qualify for the semi-finalist group of 11,000. The selection process is then broadened to include the recommendations of teachers and principals, the academic record of the candidate, his extracurricular activities, and finally, his scores on the Scholastic Aptitude Test.

It is clear that the high initial cut-off point on the Qualifying Test means that the National Merit Scholarship program is not having a great deal of effect measured in terms of making it possible for students who would not otherwise have gone to attend college. Despite the fact that the size of the stipend is related to the individual's need, this is an extraordinarily bright and accomplished group of young people who almost certainly would have

[1] The National Merit Scholarship Corporation was established in 1955 as a result of the efforts of the Ford Foundation and Carnegie Corporation of New York.

attended college anyway.[1] Merit Scholarship stipends, however, do have a redistributive effect on the college choices of the winners, with a few select colleges getting the bulk.[2]

Problems

Despite the concern of some organizations about improving selection techniques, external testing is still creating problems which both the participating schools and the sponsors will have to solve in the near future. These can be summarized under three main headings: (1) the duplication of effort and the problem of time as external testing programs multiply, (2) the problem of making the best use of test scores, and (3) the effects of external testing on school curricula and teaching methods.

Duplication of Effort. Research has indicated that most of the scholastic aptitude tests used in external testing programs are sampling abilities from the same general universe; that is, they are measuring the same thing. Even the tests which are oriented heavily in the direction of achievement correlate highly with commonly used measures of verbal and mathematical aptitude. That this is so is not surprising. The chances are that the high school student with high scholastic aptitude will have learned more than the lower ability student and will consequently do well on achievement tests. But the high correlation between tests used by different external testing programs implies that there is considerable duplication of effort during the last two years of high school when some students may take as many as half a dozen different tests. If, as is suggested by the recent publication on testing published by the American Association of School Administrators,[3] any one of these tests would tell as much about the

[1] It is also worth noting that the NMS program, by drawing attention to the 25,000 students who do not receive Merit Scholarship awards, but who did well on the examination, frequently causes these students to receive other offers of scholarship aid.

[2] By 1960, 341 Merit Scholars had elected to attend Harvard University. The college enrolling the next largest number was Massachusetts Institute of Technology with 233. In third place was Radcliffe College, which is now awarding a Harvard diploma, with 103.

[3] American Association of School Administrators, Council of Chief State School Officers, National Association of Secondary School Principals, *Testing, Testing, Testing*. Washington, 1962.

student's scholarship as any other one, what is the justification for the additional expenditures of time and effort on the part of both students and school administrators?

There are some arguments in support of the current duplication of effort in external testing. In the first place, having the opportunity to take several tests in the competition for scholarships and college admissions relieves some of the "last chance" anxiety on the part of the student. The alternative to the present situation would be to centralize all scholarship and admissions selection with reference to one or two tests which might increase the pressure on the student to the breaking point. Having a bad day would be fatal, and failure would be complete and final. In addition, the substitution of one or two tests for the present multiplicity would remove even the possibility that the tests might measure different abilities of individuals.

A frequently overlooked fact in discussions about external testing is that the amount of student time spent in taking external tests is certainly far less than the time spent in numerous other school activities, most of which are less closely related to the serious business of education than is testing: athletics, the senior play, the school yearbook, the home economics club, cheerleading, the marching band, and so on. All of these activities are worthwhile for many reasons, but it has been pointed out by several testers that it is inconsistent to complain about the two or three days a year that children lose from their studies because of testing (which at least has some relevance to intellectual pursuits) when most high school seniors lose far more days as a result of football practice or the school glee club. John Stalnaker, president of the National Merit Scholarship Corporation, argues that one of the important functions of the many external testing programs is to draw some attention to intellectual achievement, which, after all, is the primary reason for schools.

Another point in favor of having more than a few external testing programs is that test-taking, like any other activity requires practice. We have considerable evidence to support the contention that scores improve somewhat with repeated exposure to standardized tests. Familiarity with tests may therefore be a justification not only for external testing, but also for a certain amount of internal testing throughout the school experience of the child. As long as tests are going to be used in selection processes (and until something better comes along this is likely), it makes sense to familiarize children with the general form of the problems they will have to solve on such tests.

The ethics of practicing to take tests and thereby "spuriously" improving one's score may have its analogue in the problem facing the theater patron when someone shouts "fire." It is obviously dangerous and dysfunctional for the group as a whole to run to the exits in panic. On the other hand, if there is going to be a stampede for the exit, the best course of action for the individual is to get there first. Similarly, in the case of testing, if some people are going to have the advantage of familiarity with tests, the only sensible course of action is to encourage everyone to have the same experience, thus nullifying any unfair advantage on the part of a particular group. The Educational Testing Service has taken this course in advising high school juniors to take the Preliminary Scholastic Aptitude Test primarily for guidance purposes, but also to get experience in taking tests of this type. Many college applicants also take the Scholastic Aptitude Test twice. Aside from the value of practice, taking a standardized test is usually an educational experience. Not only is knowledge about oneself gained, but like any intellectual enterprise, taking an aptitude or achievement test may stimulate interest in subject matter, increase the ability of the student to think clearly, and add to knowledge in general.

It is clear that, with respect to time and effort, there is some justification for having as many external testing programs as we have at present. There is probably a limit, however, and many critics have argued that we have passed it already. Some consolidation in testing may be feasible at present without any loss in the diversity of tests offered or in the adequacy of student preparation for standardized tests. Some trends in this direction are already discernible. The National Merit Scholarship Corporation and the College Scholarship Service run by the Educational Testing Service for the College Entrance Examination Board were established to enable organizations having funds for scholarships to make use of established scholarship testing program for evaluating candidates instead of having to set up their own program. In addition, an increasing number of external testing programs are being designed to take place completely outside of the school on weekends and in some other location, so as not to interfere with school activities.

While it is not realistic or even advisable to recommend that school administrators forbid or discourage student participation in external scholarship and admissions testing programs, educators at the state and local level can help to eliminate those testing programs that presently serve no useful purpose. School systems may also find that it is unnecessary to attempt a heavy schedule of internal standardized testing during the last years of high school when externally sponsored programs are most prevalent.

Use of External Test Results. Ensuring that test results are used wisely, however, is a much more formidable problem than guarding against overtesting. The question of what ability tests measure will be examined in Chapter VI, but it has been pointed out by Henry Dyer of Educational Testing Service,[1] among others, that standardized tests generally provide less reliable and valid information about an individual's capabilities than most people who use tests realize. Not only are the scores of a single individual likely to fluctuate between tests, but even if standardized tests were perfectly reliable (that is, the same individual always got the same score on the same test), it is likely that, except for a moderate correlation with academic performance over a short period of time, tests are relatively poor predictors of long-range success.[2]

At best then, a test score ought to be viewed as indicating a range of scores within which the individual's "true" score probably falls, and it should be evaluated only in the light of other information about the individual. Unfortunately, since many external testing programs have been set up to sort out large numbers of candidates for college admission or scholarship aid, test scores do not always receive the skeptical, probabilistic treatment that they deserve. The result is often an overreliance on the accuracy and meaning of the score. Not all test users are ignorant of these facts (and the number that are is diminishing), but con-

[1] See Dyer, Henry, "On the Reduction of Ignorance About Tests in Guidance." Lecture given at the Guidance Institute, Hunter College, New York, July 14, 1959.

[2] See Chapter VII for a discussion of the problems of long-range prediction.

venience and necessity may become the parents of inflexibility, with the result that test scores are used inappropriately.

We see evidence of a possible overdependence on test scores in the Merit Scholarship program cut-off point at the 98th percentile. The justification in this case is that about 11,000 finalists is the maximum number that can be given a thoroughgoing evaluation, and the only practical way to reduce the original field of 500,000 to this more manageable number is to take the top 11,000 test scores. The argument is further bolstered by pointing out that while not perfect it is the fairest way of making the cut. Furthermore, it is argued that this group of 11,000 top-scorers probably includes virtually all the individuals we would have selected had we looked carefully at every one of the original 500,000.

It is this latter assumption that bears closer scrutiny and that demands careful research by psychometricians and test users. The only real basis for complaining about a particular use of test scores is that the present method misses better candidates than it selects. If the method used results in the best possible individuals being chosen, certainly we have no cause for alarm. But critics of external testing have frequently pointed out that so rigid a use of test scores violates most of the principles of testing and precludes the identification of many potentially able students, such as the talented but onesided individual or the particularly creative person. This latter problem has concerned the National Merit Scholarship Corporation greatly and the research staff of the Corporation has been constantly engaged in the search for ways to identify the uniquely talented individual who does not look like the typical Merit Scholar. A result of this research was the recent initiation of an experimental program in which 84 Merit Scholarships went to semi-finalists whose abilities did not fit the standard mold but who displayed exceptional talent in a particular area or unusual motivation in the face of handicapping circumstances. These students will be followed throughout their college career by the research group at National Merit Scholarship Corporation and their performance evaluated in relation to winners selected according to the typical criteria.

Effects on Curriculum. The last and possibly most serious issue stemming from the spread of external testing programs is their effect on curriculum and teaching methods. A standardized test, whether it be internally or externally sponsored, measures not only the abilities of the student who takes it, but also the resources of the educational institution responsible for that individual's training. An exceptional performance, even on a scholastic aptitude test, reflects not only on the student but also on his teachers and the total learning environment. That this should be so is inevitable. Teachers and administrators will always have an interest in how well their students do, and it is likely that parents will continue to hold the school responsible, at least in some measure, for the performance of their children. In the case of internal testing, the tests are selected by the teacher or the school administrator and they are used primarily for the benefit of the school; scores may not even be reported to parents, and summary statistics are not usually published comparing teachers, classes, or schools. Since the school is giving the test, the pressure is almost solely on the student and the share of the blame or credit held by the school is proportionately less.

But the stakes are much higher in the case of an externally administered test. The school, the teacher, and the student are being evaluated together. This joint responsibility increases as external testing programs move in the direction of achievement-oriented tests, which clearly measure both the learning ability of the student and the teaching ability of the teacher.[1] It is only natural, therefore, that teachers and administrators alike should do their best to prepare children for external tests. If school officials were not already inclined in this direction, parents would force such a policy because of the rewards being offered for success on the tests.

The amount of preparation possible for a standardized test varies considerably with the test. It is extremely difficult to prepare for a verbal or mathematical aptitude test. Studies of the effects of coaching courses and other cram sessions on College Board Scholastic Aptitude Test (SAT) scores indicate that it

[1] Officials of the National Merit Scholarship Corporation have stated that NMSC would like to move farther in the direction of achievement measures in the Qualifying Test, but that such a development is virtually impossible inasmuch as it would imply comparisons between schools that would make schools reluctant to participate in the program.

takes an enormous amount of effort to affect grades significantly, if it is possible to change them at all.[1] Aptitude tests scores, however, are almost certainly influenced by the general excellence of the school curriculum, its educational resources, and its teachers. While it may not be possible to change SAT scores by cramming, no one denies that the SAT contains a measure of learning in addition to innate mental ability.

It is reasonable to believe that achievement test scores are somewhat more subject, in general, to the influence of special preparation; in addition, they are likely to reflect the relationship between the curriculum offerings of a particular school and the information demands of the test. These facts mean that tests may have a significant influence on the subject matter being presented in schools. It is important to point out that this influence may not be altogether harmful. There is much unsystematic evidence which suggests that tests have played an important role in raising standards and improving the quality of the educational system in the United States as a whole. On the other hand, traditionally we have revolted at the thought of any external agency having control over the curriculum or teaching methods being used by the local school system, and we now find that a variety of *ad hoc* agencies are exerting an undetermined amount of influence on the kinds of things that are being taught at the local level, as well as on the way they are being taught. Probably the best example of the dangers of this influence is the case of the Regents' Examinations in New York State. Achievement on the externally administered Regents' Examinations has traditionally been used as the criterion of school and individual success in New York State. The result has been that high school teachers in New York public schools spend much of their time preparing students for these

[1] In 1960 the Trustees of the College Entrance Examination Board, on the basis of several intensive studies of the effects of special coaching courses on the Scholastic Aptitude Test, made the following statement: "The evidence collected leads us to conclude that intensive drill for the Scholastic Aptitude Test does not yield gains in scores large enough to affect decisions made by colleges with respect to the admission of students. Of the two parts of the test, the Verbal part seems almost totally insensitive to drill, while the Mathematical part for some groups may, with effort, be raised by so little, perhaps an average of 25 points on a 600 point scale, that it is not reasonable to believe that admissions decisions are allowed to turn on such slender differences. It is important to note that the tests are merely supplementary to the school record and other evidence taken into account by admission officers." *College Entrance Examination Report, 1957–1959*, p. 136.

tests, basically by drilling pupils on copies of tests used in previous years.

The Regents' Examinations in New York probably have had the beneficial effect of raising standards throughout the state, but many have argued that they have also had the unanticipated effect of setting limits on the achievement of students through a stagnation in the development of new teaching methods, and in unwillingness of school officials to experiment with curriculum innovations.

In a recent report to the New York State Commissioner of Education on the subject of Regents' Examinations, Dr. Henry M. Brickell,[1] a special consultant to the Commissioner, criticized the Regents' Examinations program and advised its discontinuation at least for a trial period, in order to stimulate innovation in educational techniques and thereby revitalize the state educational system. Most other states that have established state testing programs (for example, California) have elected to permit local school systems to select their own tests and administer them internally, thus removing the potential straitjacketing effect of external mandatory testing.

There are indications that both testing agencies and school officials are becoming aware of these problems. In the most recent Annual Report of the Educational Testing Service, its president, Henry Chauncey, pointed out that substantial gains have been made recently in the art of preparing achievement test questions which require more than purely factual knowledge of the subject matter. The new questions require students to reason, to use data provided, and to apply their factual knowledge to the solution of new problems. This "transfer of training" requirement makes it more difficult to cram for achievement tests by rote memorization of large quantities of factual material. While such questions may not lessen the impact of external testing programs on the kinds of courses and subject matter required of high school students, they may at least permit some innovation in teaching techniques, with the result that students have not only a

[1] Brickell, Henry M., *Organizing New York State for Educational Change:* A Report to the State Commissioner of Education. State Department of Education, Albany, N. Y., 1962.

mastery of factual information but also an ability to apply this information in new and different ways. It also should be pointed out that the potential impact of tests on curriculum content is another point in favor of having more than one external testing program, with each stressing somewhat different areas of learning and competence.

The effect of testing on curriculum and teaching methods is another area in which research findings are urgently needed. We need to know to what extent teachers are "teaching to the test" and how much administrators are tailoring curricula to match test requirements. We must be able to tell when we have overstepped the narrow boundary between the setting of standards and the stifling of initiative. Without research on these questions, most of the arguments and counter-arguments about the effects of external testing are not resolvable.

SUMMARY

The use of standardized ability tests by schools for guidance, grouping, and evaluation (both academic and nonacademic) and by other organizations for purposes of selection, admissions, and standard setting is widespread in American society. All of the information presently available indicates that at least three-quarters of the public school systems in the United States and a large proportion of the independent schools have regular internal testing programs and that most of the remainder make use of tests to some extent. Our data also show that more than a dozen national school or college testing programs are currently in existence, in addition to external testing sponsored by numerous state and local agencies. Internal testing seems to occur somewhat more frequently at the elementary grade levels, while external testing programs are typically encountered from junior high school grades through college. The American child who has not had the experience of taking one or more standardized ability, intelligence, aptitude, or achievement tests, by the time he finishes high school is becoming an increasingly rare species.

While it is not always clear just how test results are being used, either by schools for internal purposes or by external organizations in the process of making decisions about students, there is little disagreement that tests frequently play an important part in a wide range of decisions which may critically affect the lives of young people in the society. It is also likely that tests have an effect on the aspirations and expectations of children and their parents.

These facts lead us to the conclusion that testing has become an important factor in American education not only from the standpoint of the child and his parents, but also from the point of view of the school or college. Neither the student nor the administrator can any longer afford to overlook ability testing or be indifferent to the test results. This is as it should be, since the value of standardized testing is directly related to the interest and diligence with which the results are interpreted. If we are to make the most of our testing technology in improving our educational system, our greatest hope lies in research rather than invective, in careful evaluation instead of emotional outburst, and in a realization that while we have come a long way, there is an even greater distance to go.

V

Testing in Business and Industry, Government, and the Military

In preceding chapters we presented an overview of current testing practices in the United States; in addition, we examined educational uses of ability tests in some detail. In this chapter the discussion will be extended to include testing by business and industry, the government (including the federal civilian service as well as state and local merit systems), and the armed forces. It should be noted, however, that ability tests are used by other groups and organizations as well. Custodial institutions (both penal and rehabilitative) and a variety of professional groups are cases in point. The former use tests for diagnosis and classification, and the latter make extensive use of ability tests in establishing uniform standards of practice and in licensing potential practitioners; for example, the State Bar Associations, the United States Public Health Service, medical groups, and the New York State Psychological Association. In addition, the fairly extensive use of ability tests by private clinicians for vocational counseling and the treatment of character disorders should be mentioned.

TESTING IN BUSINESS AND INDUSTRY

An estimate of ways in which standardized tests are being used in industry must be, at best, an extremely tentative statement. In the first place, every business firm has its own way of handling personnel problems and most firms are not inclined to share these methods with their competitors or the general public. Commercial organizations, being private in ownership and management, tend to keep procedures and policies to themselves. Secondly, it is difficult to get a clear picture of industrial testing because of the tremendous diversity of practice. Not only do companies as a whole vary with respect to testing, but frequently testing practices are different in the various branches, divisions, subsidiaries, and even departments of a single firm. One personnel man may rely heavily on tests, while another in the same company will have nothing to do with testing or will tend to disregard test scores. The result is that, in the absence of a stated company policy on testing, it is extremely difficult to evaluate the impact of standardized tests on personnel selection, even where tests are widely administered.

Business and industrial testing is essentially one-sided. The test's primary function is to benefit the company, not the individual. Standardized tests are used almost solely by personnel managers in order to increase their knowledge of the capabilities of a job applicant, or the qualifications of an employee being considered for promotion or transfer. The aim is to produce a better match between job requirements and the capabilities of the available personnel. To the extent that being placed in a position that requires the use of one's abilities is beneficial to the subject, one may gain from being tested, but the rationale for industrial testing is the company's potential gain in productivity as a result of making maximum use of personnel resources.

The only exception to this predominantly utilitarian approach is the ability testing which is done by some management consultant or executive recruiting services. There are several companies that operate as combination employment agencies and high-level vocational counselors, and use tests not only to evaluate the qualifications of their clients, but also to provide a basis for advising the individual as to the most advantageous career path for him. The amount of testing done by such firms is small relative to the mass of industrial personnel testing and is limited to a select group of individuals.

Extent of Industrial Testing

Although the evidence is fragmentary, it is fairly clear that a large number of industrial firms in the United States make use of standardized tests in selecting, promoting, or transferring personnel. In response to a 1960 Harvard Business School questionnaire survey of industrial testing,[1] more than 50 per cent of the companies that replied (which, however, comprised only 34 per cent of the total number of those sent questionnaires) indicated that they were then using tests in personnel selection.

Moreover, this study revealed a positive relationship between size of company and the likelihood of reporting frequent use of tests in personnel selection and promotion. Sixty per cent of the reporting companies with over 10,000 employees stated that they used tests frequently as an aid in selecting salaried employees, while only 34 per cent of the reporting companies with fewer than 100 employees used tests for the same purpose. In the selection of nonsalaried personnel, the corresponding figures are 52 per cent of the largest companies and 20 per cent of the smallest companies.

Slightly more than a third (36 per cent) of the largest companies reported that they frequently used tests as an aid in promoting or transferring salaried employees, while only 19 per cent of the smallest companies reported this use of tests. For hourly employees, the figures are 24 per cent and 7 per cent for large and small companies, respectively. These data indicate that the impact of testing is probably greater than the percentage for the total sample would imply since the large companies make the greatest use of tests. In addition to the fact that personnel policies in small companies may be on a somewhat more informal basis, this difference between large and small companies is probably due generally to a lack of testing specialists in small companies and lower expenditures for personnel work.

It should be noted that the criterion for the numbers presented above was "frequent" use of tests, and this term may have been interpreted in different ways by different company respondents to the questionnaire. In any case, the companies that use tests seldom or infrequently, or only in specialized personnel areas, should not be overlooked. As was pointed out elsewhere, the Psychological Corporation reported that better than 90 per cent of the 500 largest companies in the United States purchased tests from the Corporation during the past five years. This supports the

[1] Ward, Lewis B., "Putting Executives to the Test," *Harvard Business Review*, vol. 38, July-August, 1960, pp. 6 ff.

contention that testing is considerably more common on the part of larger companies.

Lewis' article in the *Harvard Business Review* also makes the point that testing has been on the increase during the past ten years, contrary to the belief of some observers that business has become discouraged with psychological testing. While there is evidence that many firms have been disappointed with the results of their testing program,[1] perhaps because they expected too much, it appears that industrial testing is on the increase. A survey conducted by the National Industrial Conference Board in 1954 found that at that time only 27 per cent of the largest companies were making substantial use of tests, and only 43 per cent of all companies. The operational definition of "substantial" may not coincide with the definition of "frequently" but the difference between the percentages reported in 1954 and 1960 is so large that evidence favors the position that testing has increased, particularly on the part of large companies.

In addition to personnel departments of large firms that carry on testing programs, it has been estimated[2] that there are more than 200 and possibly as many as 1,000 independent consulting firms in the United States offering psychological services, including testing. Although many of these are small, one-man organizations, they represent a significant part of the total sales of standardized test instruments. These firms either purchase tests from publishers, such as the Psychological Corporation, that specialize in test development or publish their own tests.

Problems in Industrial Testing

The use of standardized testing in evaluating personnel in business and industry has been the subject of considerable controversy. We pointed out that one of the reasons for the early enthusiasm for testing on the part of business leaders was the increasing technological complexity of the society, which made it more important for companies to select the right man for a given

[1] *Ibid.*, p. 15.

[2] See Whyte, William H., Jr., "The Fallacies of Personality Testing," *Fortune*, September, 1954, pp. 117–121; and French, Wendell L., "Consulting Firm Responsibility in Reporting Test Validation Studies," *American Psychologist*, vol. 16, April, 1961, pp. 145–148.

job. As industrial organizations have grown in size, the task of recruiting and evaluating personnel has become a full-time job in itself. Standardized tests at first looked like the answer to the prayers of the harassed personnel manager who found himself making many decisions about the technical qualifications of applicants for jobs with which he might not be personally familiar. And these decisions have become more and more important as the competition for talented technicians, engineers, and creative executives has grown stiffer. Even at the level of the employee on an hourly wage, the number of skilled jobs has increased steadily and the problem of evaluating an individual's competence has consequently become more important.

While ability tests may have paid dividends in increased efficiency and overall quality of employees, in many cases tests have been a mixed blessing. Personnel experts have found that tests are not infallible and not infrequently are more trouble than they are worth. The most serious drawback to testing from the point of view of the business firm is the difficulty in predicting performance in jobs requiring abilities that are hard to define and, consequently, to test (as for example, most administrative and executive positions). The problem of developing tests that will identify individuals who will turn out to be outstanding executives, scientists, or engineers, continues to be one of the most challenging tasks facing psychometricians and personnel specialists alike. A more detailed analysis of some of the factors involved in the prediction of performance at high levels of ability is included in Chapter VII, but it is worth noting here that the crux of the problem is the difficulty in deciding just what is required for success as a businessman, scientist, or engineer. Probably some minimum level of intelligence is necessary, but beyond this we know little about what goes into creativity or business acumen. Furthermore, we admit that successful executives display a variety of styles of behavior.[1]

[1] In an effort to take into account some of the social and personality factors in business success, and also to identify individuals with personality problems and character disorders, many personnel departments make use of personality tests in the selection process despite a general lack of demonstrated validity. While the Harvard survey figures do not distinguish between personality and ability tests, data from test publishers indicate that industrial personnel departments are an important

The competitive nature of business firms leads to further complications in the usefulness of standardized tests as devices for personnel evaluation. Competition tends to produce a reluctance on the part of personnel specialists to discuss their techniques in public or in front of their competitors for fear that their methods may be stolen. This tendency toward secrecy, combined with the business orientation of utilitarianism, results in a general lack of publications reporting new testing techniques devised by industrial psychologists or attempts to test the validity of existing measurement instruments.[1] As a consequence, each company tends to go its own way and make mistakes without having the benefit of the experience of other companies in comparable situations. In cases where business firms either do not have, or choose not to allocate, funds for research on the effectiveness of the tests they are using, intuition frequently replaces empirically established validity, and the result is virtually no control over the way tests are used or interpreted. Many companies attempt to avoid these problems by turning their testing over to a commercial agency specializing in test development or to one of the many consulting firms. However, more and more large companies are developing their own tests, administering them, and interpreting the scores without external interference or assistance.

Another obstacle which must be overcome if industrial testing is to live up to its promise is organized labor's objection to the use of tests in the selection and promotion of union members. It is ironical that in the one area where tests have proved their effectiveness, in the selection of skilled workers as well as individuals desiring clerical and similar jobs, personnel departments have frequently been prevented from making use of tests by

---

market for personality tests, including both projective (for example, The Rorschach Ink Blot Test, The Thematic Apperception Test) and nonprojective types (for example, The Minnesota Multiphasic Personality Inventory).

While personality tests may help to identify the abnormal individual sufficiently to justify their use, William H. Whyte's instructions for cheating on personality tests in *The Organization Man* illustrate some of the pitfalls of depending heavily on such tests to reveal a great deal about the examinee. One of the important problems still to be solved by those who are working on new ways of measuring such elusive qualities as creativity, social skill, and personality adjustment is the development of a test on which the examinee cannot cheat.

[1] See, for example, French, Wendell L., *op. cit.* A rebuttal to French's statement by Martin M. Bruce, a consulting psychologist, appears in the *American Psychologist,* vol. 16, October, 1961, pp. 651–652.

unions, because the latter look upon tests as a potential threat to their control over hiring, firing, and promotion.

We may conclude that industrial and business testing occupies a somewhat uncertain position in personnel management, but that most companies are not ready to give up on tests as an aid in the selection and allocation of manpower. The problem of predicting high level executive performance with either personality or ability tests has not yet been solved satisfactorily, and although psychometricians, personnel consultants, and management alike are aware of the difficulties, approaches to this problem have thus far been largely unsystematic and uncoordinated. In the areas where psychometricians are on firmer ground, in the measurement of specific abilities and skills, organized labor has slowed down the application of existing testing technology.

While there is evidence that standardized tests are being administered in larger and larger numbers, there are also indications that in some instances tests are being given with the philosophy that "they won't do any harm" and the scores, more often than not, may be disregarded. A contributing factor here is the relative lack of communication throughout the business world concerning new developments in selection techniques and the lack of coordination in the research which is done.

TESTING IN GOVERNMENT

With the continued expansion of government at all levels—federal, state, and local—personnel selection has become a problem of major importance. In 1959, 8,127,000 people were employed by government agencies in the United States, excluding the military, of whom more than two million were civilian employees of the federal government. Since 1930 the number of civilians working for the federal government has quadrupled[1] and there is no evidence that we have reached the peak of this growth. In the light of these figures, it is apparent that the success of our democratic government and the progress of the country as a whole depends in part on the efficiency of these government agencies, as well as on their continued responsibility

[1] U.S. Bureau of Labor Statistics figures, reported in *The World Almanac, 1961.* New York World-Telegram, publisher, pp. 684, 755, 756.

to the people they serve. A central government employing two million people, not counting the armed forces, occupies a position of tremendous influence in the society. This influence may be either beneficial or detrimental to the society, depending as much on the capabilities of the people administering the power as on the policies that provide the guidelines. History has provided us with many examples of corrupt and incompetent government bureaucracies that have helped to destroy the society they were supposed to serve.

Government personnel policies, therefore, have a direct influence on the welfare of the country as a whole. As the influence of government spreads, the importance of these policies increases concomitantly. There are two main processes by which personnel can be, and are, recruited by federal, state, and local governments. Government jobs may be filled either on the basis of political affiliation (the "spoils" system) or of merit.[1] Theoretically, these two alternatives are not mutually exclusive, but in practice an absolute distinction usually must be made in order to preserve the identity of each.[2] While the ability of political appointees certainly is considered in the process of job allocation, a more important criterion is frequently the amount of support rendered in a political campaign. The rationale for the existence of political patronage is the necessity of motivating individuals to take part in political activity, both from a financial standpoint and a personal standpoint. The dangers of the spoils system if extended willy-nilly are, of course, the possibility that a single party might acquire too much political power, or that important administrative jobs might be filled with mediocre or incompetent individuals. Regardless of the functions and dysfunctions of political patronage, the trend at most levels of government in the United States has been away from political appointments and toward the establishment of merit systems based either on open

[1] At the time when federal grant-in-aid regulations first required states to adopt merit system principles and implement them with a merit system organization, several states at first resisted this move. The governor of one state attempted to reconcile these two methods of selection by pointing out that he "believed in merit but he believes his friends have more merit than his enemies." See Aronson, Albert H., "Merit Systems in Grant-in-Aid Programs," *Public Personnel Review*, vol. 17, October, 1956, pp. 231–237.

[2] The procedure that results in an appointment to the United States Military Academy at West Point is a good example of a combination of "spoils" and "merit," which appears to work extremely well.

competition for jobs or the establishment of minimum qualifications.

Selection on the Basis of Merit

The merit system in the United States began with the creation of the U.S. Civil Service Commission through an act of Congress in 1883 and has since spread to the state and local levels, partly as a result of state and local initiatives and partly as a result of federal pressure. At the present time, the overwhelming majority of government jobs in the United States are filled on the basis of merit, and while the various programs are not perfect in their conception or operation, for the most part they are based on the same set of objectives.

In 1959 the U.S. Civil Service Commission described the federal merit system as "a complete system of personnel selection and management resting on an integrated set of personnel policies, procedures, and practices designed to accomplish three basic objectives."[1] These objectives are (1) to recruit a competent work force, (2) to ensure a stable work force, and (3) to provide equal opportunity for employment. The first of these aims, recruiting a competent work force, requires not only that efforts be made to select the best qualified job applicants, but also to attract candidates possessing the desired qualifications. The latter requirement is as important as the use of merit criteria for selection since, in order to have any real effect, the selection device must actually be used to choose one of several qualified candidates. If there is only one candidate, merit selection becomes meaningless.[2]

Ensuring a stable work force is necessary in order that the affairs of government may be conducted efficiently and without undue interruptions, despite changes in the political leadership. It has been pointed out that an important factor in this stability is the confidence of political leaders in the ability and willingness of this work force to carry out the policies established by officials responsible for policy formation. Such confidence, in turn, is

[1] U. S. Civil Service Commission, *How People Are Recruited, Examined, and Appointed in the Competitive Civil Service:* A Report Prepared for the Sub-Committee on Civil Service, Committees on Post Office and Civil Service, United States House of Representatives. Government Printing Office, Washington, p. 1, April, 1959.

[2] The implications of this point for testing practice in general will be discussed below.

created by personnel selection on the basis of ability rather than political affiliation.

Finally, a merit system seeks to provide substantially equal opportunity for employment to all interested citizens without discrimination on political, racial, religious, or other similar grounds. According to the objectives of the federal merit system, "every citizen who seeks employment by his Government has a right to be considered for it solely on the basis of his merit and fitness."[1]

The success of a merit system is based on two main characteristics, open competitive examining and a career employment system. "Open competitive examining" implies the following elements: adequate publicity, so that all interested persons can learn of the job opening; opportunity to apply, which implies that a reasonable length of time be given for application; equal and impartial application of standards, selection from among the most competent, which implies ranking of candidates in order of their relative ability and selecting from among those considered most competent; knowledge of the results (the applicant is entitled to be informed of the results of his examination), and finally, an opportunity for review (the applicant must be given an opportunity to request and receive an administrative review if he believes the standards were not properly applied in his case).

With these characteristics in mind, along with the growth of the government personnel problems, standardized, objective ability testing has become the cornerstone of the operation of merit systems in this country. While the term "examining" includes the evaluation of the applicant's experience, education, and other indications of his qualifications, it also implies an objective measure of ability wherever this is appropriate. Standardized ability tests are now used as an integral part of the examining procedure for the large majority of federal, state, and local government positions that are under merit systems. This has meant the development by civil service personnel agencies of a great variety of specific tests appropriate for the many different positions in government service. While practices vary somewhat, it is probably safe to say that government agencies at virtually all levels make use of standardized tests of one sort or another in the administration of merit systems.

[1] U. S. Civil Service Commission, *op. cit.*

Federal Civilian Service Testing

The federal civilian service encompasses all the nonelective positions in all three branches of the federal government. The vast majority of these positions, 99 per cent of two and a third million employees, are in the executive branch, and approximately 86 per cent of all federal government positions are in the competitive service; that is, they are filled through open competitive civil service examinations. Close to two million jobs, therefore, are directly subject to the rules and regulations of the U.S. Civil Service Commission, which provides a common body of personnel policies and practices for all the positions in the competitive service. With the exception of a very small number (fewer than 500) of high level scientific or professional positions (covered under Public Law 313) and an even smaller number of positions for hearing examiner, all of the jobs must be filled through open competitive examinations.

For each of the positions under its jurisdiction, the Civil Service Commission is responsible for establishing standards for the classification of jobs, as well as for the qualifications of people to fill the jobs. In carrying out these responsibilities the Commission develops different methods for examining and ranking candidates, depending on the specific requirements of the position to be filled. In many cases a written aptitude test may be used in the examination, while in other instances a performance test (for example, a test which requires the applicant to use physical equipment) is used in addition to, or in place of, the written test. Ratings of training and experience are usually prescribed as part of the examination and, less frequently, interviews and oral tests of ability are utilized.[1]

[1] With respect to personality tests, the following statement appears in a Commission memorandum on the use of tests in public personnel selection: "The Commission recognizes that significant improvements in the prediction of job adjustment may result from the development of methods of this kind, and, therefore, supports some research and keeps in touch with promising developments in other organizations. However, it recognizes that at the present stage of development, these methods, as a group, are of little practical value in public personnel selection since not enough is known about those personnel characteristics necessary to success in specific positions, and available methods are difficult to score, to interpret, and to control against intentional distortion by applicants." U. S. Civil Service Commission, "The Use of Tests by the U.S. Civil Service Commission in Public Personnel Selection." Dittoed memorandum, November, 1959.

An examination is referred to as "assembled" if a written or performance test is required; that is, for an assembled examination, a person must go to some examination point where he assembles with other competitors to take the written or performance test. No ability tests are required in "unassembled" examinations, in which case appointment is based entirely on the candidate's experience, education, or other qualifications. Objective ability tests are used in an "assembled" examination (1) if written or performance tests are available in the existing pool of testing materials that accurately measure the particular skill, knowledge, or ability needed; (2) in the event that no appropriate tests are available, if one can be developed within the time limitations imposed by the necessity of filling the particular job; (3) if a sufficient number of competitors is expected to justify the expense of using a test or developing a new test, and (4) if the need for personnel is not so great or qualified people so scarce, that even the minor delays and administrative problems involved in the use of written tests cannot be tolerated.

In the fiscal year 1958, about 60 per cent of the total number of federal civilian service examinations included written or performance tests. More than 2,000,000 tests are required annually to allow for the variety of positions covered and for the use of more than a single test when needed in examining for particular positions.

Total Examining Volume, Fiscal Year 1958[1]

	Assembled	*Unassembled*	*Total*
Examination announcements issued	4,545	2,510	7,055
Number of new hires	119,189	87,224	206,413

Scores on tests may be used in several ways: as the sole basis for the competitor's final rating, as a contributing factor in the competitor's rating, or merely as a determinant of eligibility for further consideration. In the last case, once the test has been passed, the score does not enter into the final rating. In any

[1] Reprinted from *How People Are Recruited, Examined, and Appointed in the Competitive Civil Service.* U.S. Civil Service Commission, April, 1959, p. 29.

assembled examination, however, the competitor is required to make a passing score in order to be considered eligible.

As has been pointed out above, objective tests are most appropriately used as part of the selection process for the entry and intermediate levels of professional, technical, and administrative occupations because by the time an individual has reached a more advanced level, regardless of the field, there are generally other more appropriate means for assessing his competence, such as his employment record, experience, and personal references. Federal civilian service testing can be broken down into five major areas, corresponding to different occupational groupings. The five areas include: (1) trades, skills, and clerical occupations, (2) administrative and management positions, (3) areas of professional competence, such as engineering and accounting, (4) cooperative work-study training programs for high school graduates, and (5) research and development work in scientific fields. In addition to these occupational areas, the Civil Service Commission administers tests designed to predict a candidate's ability to pass the military academy entrance tests in order that congressmen may screen applicants.

Trades, Skills, and Clerical Occupations. The jobs for which tests are most often used are in the skilled, semi-skilled, and clerical occupations, for example, stenographers and typists, office machine operators, clerks, apprentices, nursing assistants, and postal employees. Tests for these positions vary according to the skill and aptitude required. They are usually job-related in their content. The stenographer and typist test, for example, consists of a general test of word definitions, spelling, alphabetizing, grammar, arithmetic, and paragraph reading, along with performance tests in typing and shorthand. Other job-related tests are used for trades and industrial jobs, and aptitude tests may be used for recruiting inexperienced persons for training in many of these occupations.

Administrative and Management Positions. Administrative and management positions requiring individuals with college level abilities are currently filled through the Federal Service Entrance Examination. The Federal Service Entrance Examination is a single test similar to the Scholastic Aptitude Test of the College

Entrance Examination Board. It is used for screening all college graduates and other individuals of "college-calibre" who are interested in administrative careers with the federal government, regardless of the specific area of their interest (excluding such specialists as engineers and physicists). One of the major initial objectives of the Federal Service Entrance Examination was to make it easier for college graduates and others having similar ability to apply for jobs with the federal government by eliminating over 100 separate tests previously used in examining candidates for administrative positions. At present, over 100,000 candidates take the Federal Service Entrance Examination annually. It is given about six times during the school year and is administered throughout the United States and its territories at more than 1,000 examination points.

An additional feature of the Federal Service Entrance Examination program is the identification of exceptionally able candidates for appointment as management interns. Management interns receive special training in government administration and management and therefore are in demand for the best entering jobs in the government service. Although everyone passing the Federal Service Entrance Examination has the same long-range career opportunities, advancement in the competitive service being dependent on merit, those individuals who qualify as management interns have an advantage over other contestants as a result of the additional intensive development training they receive and the more strategically located jobs they are likely to occupy at the start. In order to receive an appointment as a management intern, applicants must not only "pass" the general test, they are also required to pass either a test on administrative problems or a test on public affairs. The former is a test of judgment on types of problems which occur in large organizations, while the latter covers governmental and economic problems. Candidates are also screened by interviews and an intensive review of their records and references.

Professional Competence in Engineering and Accounting. Written tests are also useful in evaluating the abilities and professional qualifications of individuals having abilities in specialized areas such as engineering and accounting. In particular, applicants in the field of engineering who do not meet the full professional educational requirements are tested in order to determine whether they have a knowledge and understanding of engineering equivalent to that furnished by a full engineering course of study. Tests are also of value in furnishing some evidence of the experience of a particular employee in a position which, from the statement of duties, is difficult to identify clearly as professional or nonprofessional. Ten such tests of competence are now in use for engineering specialties and one test is available for similar use in the field of accounting.

Work Study Program. Another important use of objective tests is in connection with the student-trainee program designed to enable high school graduates to combine academic study and on-the-job training. In this program, usually of five years' duration, students alternate periods of college attendance with periods of employment. Tests of verbal ability, abstract reasoning, and, in some cases, algebra, are used to help to identify those students who are most likely to succeed. The fields covered by this program include: accounting, agricultural economics, engineering, entomology, forestry, geology, home economics, metallurgy, meteorology, oceanography, physics, plant pest control, range conservation, soil conservation, soil science, and statistics.

Entering Research Scientists. Finally, the Commission has developed a battery of tests for use in the selection of research scientists at the entering levels. This battery includes a test of the ability to formulate problems in mathematical terms and achievement tests in college level chemistry, physics, or mathematics, as the case may be.

Once an individual is a civil service employee, he may face additional tests as part of an evaluation for promotion since merit standards are enforced throughout the system. The farther the individual advances in government service, however, the less likely it is that objective tests will be used in the evaluation of his abilities unless he is being considered for a basically different type of position requiring substantially different abilities. Since this is probably a relatively rare occurrence, it may be concluded that the bulk of federal civilian service testing takes place at the entrance to government service.

In summary, objective ability tests are an integral part of the open competitive merit system which is the core of the career civilian service in the federal government. Standardized tests, both written and performance, are used at all levels in the merit system, from stenographer-typist to research scientist and professional engineer. While test scores are seldom used as the sole criterion for the applicant's rating (thereby determining his chances of employment), it is likely that they frequently play a crucial role in the selection process. The handbooks of instructions for examining boards indicate that Civil Service Commission officials are cognizant of the limitations of tests, but in fact there remains little recourse for the applicant, who for one reason or another fails to achieve a passing score, except to wait until the test is given again. The Commission has felt, therefore, a responsibility to make every effort to inform prospective applicants of the nature of the examination process and, specifically, of the kind of test that will be given. In the case of the stenographer-typist examination, for example, a free booklet has been prepared in which an entire test, instead of just sample questions, is reproduced with answer sheets and full instructions so that the candidate will be aware of what is expected. At the same time, fairly elaborate security measures are taken to ensure that no candidate will have an unfair advantage as a result of prior knowledge of the specific test questions.

Testing by State and Local Government Agencies

Most state and local governments have followed the example of the federal government in establishing merit standards for public personnel selection and in so doing have adopted methods that rely heavily on the use of standardized tests. While there is considerable variation among the many agencies serving the public at the state and local levels as to the administration of merit systems and the positions included in them, the same basic principles apply in theory at least throughout the country at all levels. In the spread of merit system principles to state and local agencies, the influence of the federal government on civil service practices has been considerable. Beginning with amendments to the Social Security Act in 1939, the federal government has required all state and local agencies receiving federal grant-in-aid funds to establish and maintain personnel standards on a merit basis. This policy, initiated in the employment security and public assistance programs under the Social Security Board, has been expanded to related health and welfare programs, and has had a pronounced effect on raising the standards of public personnel selection. Prior to 1939 only nine states had general civil service systems, and several of these were not functioning effectively. At the present time every state lists at least one merit system board or civil service commission serving a variety of state and local agencies, and many states have developed effective joint civil service programs covering all public personnel areas.

Generalizations as to the extent of testing and the uses of test scores by these agencies are difficult to make, but the majority of persons who enter public service at the state and local levels today probably face standardized tests of ability of one sort or another. The federal government has also played an important role in assisting states with the technical problems of administering merit systems, first through the State Technical Advisory Service (established by the Social Security Board) and now through the Division of State Merit Systems in the Department of Health, Education, and Welfare. According to Albert H. Aronson, its current chief, this unit has reviewed merit system organization and operations, and has advised on rules, practices, and procedures. In addition to the preparation of manuals and bulletins on merit system installation, personnel selection methods, and other aspects of the program, the Division of State Merit Systems conducts institutes on examination and classification techniques, and has made available to state agencies field consultations on the various phases of personnel administration.

The federal merit system service also constructs and compiles objective examination materials to which the states contribute through cooperative item construction projects and on which they can all draw. Most states have called for these materials each year and the federal unit has sent out to states, in response to specific requests, more than 15,000 examinations (including in all more than 800,000 multiple-choice items) for several thousand classes of positions in state agencies. This service has proved valuable in reducing the expense of setting up duplicate technical examining staffs in the grant-in-aid agencies of the states.

In general, while the record is still very uneven, public personnel selection at the state and local levels has shown marked improvement over the past two decades partly as a result of federal assistance and prompting, and partly as a result of the initiative of the local agencies themselves. Spoils system traditions are still very much in evidence, particularly in those areas where political machines influence the electoral process, but as government has grown in complexity, the sheer increase in the number of available jobs has created pressure in the direction of uniform personnel policies, at least at the lower level. An important factor in this change has been the increasing numbers of individuals who have been willing to work for the government, thereby raising the quality of personnel generally and permitting qualification standards on examinations to be set at a meaningful level. As salaries of government employees improve, this trend can be expected to continue. Government unions also are likely to play an increasingly important role in enforcing merit system principles, as the Federal Postal Workers' Union has already done.

Problems in Government Personnel Selection

Many of the problems facing merit system or civil service administrators are the same as those encountered by academic admissions officers and industrial or military personnel specialists. Defining the qualifications necessary for maximum performance, developing a valid, reliable measure of those qualifications or abilities, and finding the trained personnel to administer and interpret the test are still the main stumbling blocks encountered by all test users. Because of the rapid growth of government, these problems are multiplied by the number of jobs involved and the scarcity of experts (and funds) to carry out validation studies, and research on new tests. In view of the size of current staffs and the funds available for validation studies, it is remarkable that government personnel specialists have managed to keep up with the demand for increasing numbers of basic tests and new forms of established instruments. It is not surprising that a few tests like the stenographer-typist test and the Federal Service Entrance Examination have received the greatest emphasis and have been relatively successful. The development and validation of tests which will measure in any detail the abilities necessary for the performance of several thousand different occupations remains an enormous job.

In addition to the standard difficulties in evaluating the abilities and predicting the performance of individuals, merit system administrators must solve the problem of attracting sufficient numbers of qualified applicants to make the competitive examining system meaningful. Furthermore, the selection process must not be so time-consuming that the more capable applicants are either discouraged or take other jobs before they are notified. Only if there are more qualified applicants than there are positions, will the system continue to work in the way in which it is designed to work.

TESTING IN THE MILITARY

All of the armed services use standardized tests for screening, classifying, and selecting men in an attempt to make maximum use of available manpower. Like the federal civilian service, each of the branches of the military requires men having diverse abilities and aptitudes to fill a large number of different jobs. The Army, for example, distinguishes about 500 different occupations, from cook to radio technician, all of which require different skills. In addition to initial screening for fitness and the classification of men according to their particular aptitudes, tests are used in the selection of officer candidates and in the process of making appointments to a variety of special training schools.

Although there are many similarities between military and civilian uses of tests, there are also some important differences. Because of the unique characteristics of military organization, once a person is in the Army, Navy, or Air Force, he becomes part of a manpower pool, the members of which are available for any assignment, depending on existing needs. Unlike civilian employment, including the government civilian service, the military man cannot quit if he doesn't like his current assignment, boss, or working hours; at least not until his tour of duty expires. The result is that if the right man for the job can be found, there is less of a problem in getting him to take the position, or to stay in it as long as he is needed. This results, inevitably, in a somewhat more "manpower" oriented approach to testing as opposed to a "human development" approach, in which the important factor is making sure that the individual has an opportunity to make fullest use of his abilities. In a period of relative peace, however, problems of morale and productivity have received more and more attention, and a concerted effort has been made to increase the number of voluntary enlistments and re-enlistments in order to reduce the rate of turnover and the cost of maintaining a trained force. The result has been an increasing emphasis on the use of tests as a means of providing opportunities for Army personnel to receive specialized training or advancement in rank as an inducement to remain in the service for a longer period of time.

Another point of difference between military testing and other uses of objective tests is that military testing tends to be oriented toward the measurement of aptitude rather than achievement. There are, of course, exceptions to this rule. The Army, for example, publishes tests of proficiency in 35 different languages, including Albanian, Serbo-Croatian, Persian, and Turkish.[1] For the most part, however, there is relatively little opportunity for people to receive training in the skills required by the armed services prior to entering the particular service. There is no use, therefore, for elaborate tests to measure achievement in areas for which military service is the only source of experience or instruction; for example, piloting jet fighters.

Army Testing: An Example

The uses made of objective tests by the Army can be divided into four main categories: (1) screening in induction, enlistment, and re-enlistment; (2) initial and continued classification of enlisted personnel; (3) selection and assignment of personnel for officer training; and (4) special selection and assignment to

[1] See Personnel Research Branch, The Adjutant General's Office, U.S. Army, *Psychological Testing Programs in the U.S. Army*, July, 1959, p. 29.

Army jobs or Army job training.[1] Some of the tests and procedures used in each of these cases will be described below.

Induction, Enlistment, and Re-enlistment Screening

All male enlistees, re-enlistees, and selective service registrants, with or without prior military service, are screened for general fitness prior to induction into the Army with the Armed Forces Qualification Test (AFQT), a multiple choice examination containing separate sections for the measurement of verbal, arithmetic reasoning, and spatial relations abilities. The AFQT was developed jointly by the Army, Navy, Air Force, and Marine Corps and is used for screening purposes by all four of the services. The qualifying score on the AFQT varies somewhat, depending on the candidate's status, but in general, a percentile score of 31 or better is required for acceptance without further screening.[2] High school graduate enlistees who are applying for training in a specific area and selective service registrants who achieve a percentile score falling between 10 and 30 on the AFQT must also take the Army Classification Battery, including tests in eight different aptitude areas. The ACB will be discussed in the following section.

Selective service registrants with failing percentile scores of 0 through 9 on the AFQT are re-tested with the AFQT Verbal-Arithmetic Subtest for standby categorization in the event of full mobilization. Those scoring below 6 on the AFQT Subtest, which has a raw score range of from 0 to 30, are classified as illiterate and are then given the Nonlanguage Qualification Test (NQT), which has a raw score range of from 0 to 42. Any registrant scoring below 34 on the NQT is classified as substandard and rejected. Any applicant who fails the AFQT also takes several additional tests designed to detect deliberate failures.

Women enlistees and re-enlistees take a screening test similar to the AFQT, the Armed Forces Women's Selection Test (AFWST), and Puerto Rican selective service registrants are

[1] *Ibid.*, pp. i–iii.

[2] A percentile score of 65 is required for enlistment applicants with dependents.

given a Spanish version of the AFQT. Except in the case of the re-enlistment screening of certain categories of female personnel (principally those having dependents), whose percentile scores on the AFWST must exceed 65, the qualifying standard for women is a percentile score of 50.

It is fairly evident from these figures that AFQT screening procedures do not eliminate many candidates from eligibility for military service of one kind or another. The percentage of applicants considered to be mentally unacceptable on the basis of their test scores is about 30 per cent in the case of enlistments and less than 10 per cent in the case of draftees. This preliminary administration of objective tests, however, does make it possible to screen out the bulk of the obviously mentally incompetent. A far more refined classification of manpower on the basis of aptitude areas is then accomplished through the use of the Army Classification Battery.

Initial and Continued Classification of Enlisted Personnel

Since 1949 the Army has used a multi-aptitude classification system in the assignment of enlisted personnel to the most appropriate occupations according to their abilities. The key to the aptitude area system, as it is called, is the Army Classification Battery which is administered to all new recruits at reception stations upon induction. The ACB is currently composed of eleven separate objective tests, including the following:

Verbal Test (VE)
Arithmetic Reasoning Test (AR)
Pattern Analysis Test (PA)
Classification Inventory (CI)
Mechanical Aptitude Test (MA)
Army Clerical Speed Test (ACS)
Army Radio Code Aptitude Test (ARC)
General Information Test (GIT)
Shop Mechanics Test (SM)
Automotive Information Test (AI)
Electronics Information Test (ELI)

An enlisted man's scores on these tests are used to evaluate his aptitude in one of eight aptitude areas, and he is then assigned to an occupation on the basis of his highest aptitude area score.

Current Aptitude Area System[1]

Aptitude Area	*Component Tests*	*Occupational Areas*
Infantry-Combat	AR, CI*	Infantry Combat
Armor, Artillery & Engineers-Combat	GIT, AI	All other combat
Electronic	MA, ELI*	Electronics, Electrical Maintenance
General Maintenance	PA, SM*	Precision Maintenance, Military Crafts
Motor Maintenance	MA, AI*	Motor Maintenance
Clerical	VE, ACS*	Clerical
General Technical	VE, AR	Graphics, General Technical, Special Assignment
Radio Code	VE, ARC*	Radio Code

* Double-weighted test for given area.

Through the use of aptitude area scores, the specific abilities of the men in the manpower pool are matched with the skills and abilities required by the Army jobs that need to be filled. In the classification procedure, in addition to his aptitude area score, a thorough review is also made of each man's physical profile and work experience before the most appropriate occupational area is specified. Research has shown that the eight aptitude area scores represent combinations of abilities that are sufficiently different from one another to provide a very good chance that any man will have at least one ability score above average. On the basis of large samples of enlisted input taken from 1953 to 1958, 75 per cent of those tested with the ACB had at least one aptitude area score of 100 or higher (above average performance), which compares favorably with results from the same samples on a single general mental ability measure on which only 53 per cent scored 100 or higher.

[1] Reprinted from Human Factors Research Branch, TAG Research and Development Command, U.S. Army, Briefing Supplement, *The Aptitude Area System*. March, 1961, sec. 3.

In addition to the ACB, recruits also take a written test for the initial classification of motor vehicle drivers, the Driver Battery I, which includes a Self-Description form, a Driving Know-How Test, and an Attention to Detail Test.

The aptitude area system has proved to be of considerable value in the initial classification of enlisted men for assignment to occupations in the Army. Research continues, however, on classification instruments and procedures in an effort to improve on the current method. Specifically, research is being carried on to develop instruments that will differentiate between certain subdivisions of the present aptitude areas, for example, electronics from electrical maintenance or medical from general technical abilities. Secondly, research on personality and motivational measures has been undertaken to identify characteristics that predict what a man will do on the job as opposed to what he can do. Finally, special research is in progress to identify (1) the special capacities of men with scores below average on the AFQT, and (2) factors relating to attrition in Army training courses.

Selection and Assignment of Personnel for Officer Training

A variety of objective tests are used by the Army in the evaluation of applicants for several different officer training programs. These evaluation procedures include: (1) the selection of male and female personnel for Officer Candidate School, (2) the selection of Junior Division ROTC Graduates for Advanced ROTC training, (3) the selection of cadets for advanced ROTC training, and (4) the selection of members of regular components for admission to USMA entrance examinations.

In the selection of personnel for Officer Candidate School, an evaluation board considers the candidate's score on the Officer Candidate Test (or WAC Officer Candidate Test), along with other evidence of his leadership capabilities, and then makes a recommendation to the candidate's major commander regarding acceptance or rejection. Junior Division ROTC graduates (high school seniors) and senior division cadets (college sophomores) may qualify for advanced ROTC training by taking the General

Screening Test or the ROTC Qualifying Examination. In all of these instances an Army standard score of 115 (which corresponds roughly to the 60th percentile) on the test used is necessary unless the candidate has a record of being an "outstanding leader," in which case a standard score between 110 and 114 is acceptable.

Enlisted members of regular components of the Army or Air Force with a high school education may qualify for West Point entrance examinations by taking a prequalification battery composed of objective verbal and mathematics aptitude tests and the West Point Prequalification Inventory, which considers past performance and career motivation. Based on relative prequalification battery composite scores, approximately 150 personnel are selected to attend a Preparatory Training Facility for a period of six months prior to taking the United States Military Academy competitive entrance examinations.

Special Selection and Assignment to Army Jobs and Army Job Training

Within the Army there are a number of specialized jobs and assignments requiring abilities or aptitudes not covered specifically by the Army Classification Battery and for which Army personnel may apply and be tested at any time. These include: (1) motor vehicle driver licensing, (2) appointment to foreign language training school, (3) foreign language assignment, (4) Army recruiting duty, (5) fixed wing aviation training, and (6) helicopter pilot training.

Determining the qualifications of motor vehicle drivers for final licensing requires the administration of part 2 of the Driver Battery, which is similar to most civilian drivers' license examinations. Driver licensing and the selection of Army recruiters on the basis of sales adaptability do not involve written objective tests. For all of the other assignments mentioned, written aptitude or achievement tests are administered as part of the selection process.

Admission to Army Language School is based on the candidate's foreign language aptitude as measured by the Army Language Aptitude Test. In addition, military personnel who claim to possess a fair to good knowledge of any one of 35 foreign languages are examined with the appropriate Language Proficiency Test prior to duty assignment on the basis of their language ability. Assignment of male officer personnel and ROTC cadets to Fixed Wing Aviation School is based on the candidate's overall qualifications and his performance on the Army Aviation Test Battery, which includes a Background Inventory, Aeronautical Information Test, Mechanical Principles Test, Aircraft Orientation Test, and Flight Visualization Test. Candidates for helicopter pilot training are selected on the basis of their background and performance on the Helicopter Pilot Selection Battery, which includes an Officer Leadership Qualification Report, a Leadership Board Interview, and two objective tests, a Situational Reasoning Test and a Mechanical Principles Test.

It is clear that objective tests are used extensively by the Army in allocating personnel and in evaluating the abilities of candidates for special assignments. In most cases the individual's test score is not the sole determining factor in his acceptance, rejection, or classification, but it is likely that because of the magnitude of the selection problem faced by the Army, the number of different jobs, and the number of candidates for these jobs, tests play a considerably greater role in military personnel allocation than in other occupational areas of the society at the present time.

PART TWO
ABILITY TESTS AND PREDICTION

VI

What Ability Tests Measure

In the introduction to this monograph, we defined ability tests as instruments for the measurement of intelligence, special aptitudes, and achievement. In addition, we narrowed our present field of interest to standardized, objective ability tests. This definition, however, leaves something to be desired. Just what does an "IQ" test measure? What do we mean when we talk about ability? To what extent are abilities changeable or modifiable over time? Suppose that we can agree on a definition of "intelligence" or "mathematical aptitude," how accurately do standardized tests measure these qualities? And, even more important, of what use is such a measurement?

Although standardized testing has become widespread, complete agreement on the answers to these questions has not been reached. The following two statements, for example, made recently by highly respected behavioral scientists, are indicative of the differences of opinion which exist in regard to these issues.

> . . . it will be seen that, with the crude [intelligence] test results, taken just as they stand, nearly 23% of the total variance appears due to nongenetic influences, i.e., to environment or to unreliability, and about 77% to genetic factors; with the adjusted assessments only about 12% (or slightly more) is apparently due to nongenetic influences and 88% to genetic factors.[1]

> In view of the conceptual developments and the evidence coming from animals learning to learn, from neuropsychology and from programming electronic computers to solve problems, and from the development of intelligence in children, it would appear that intelligence should be conceived as intellectual capacities based on

[1] Burt, Cyril, "The Inheritance of Mental Ability," *American Psychologist*, vol. 13, January, 1958, p. 9.

> central processes hierarchically arranged within the intrinsic portions of the cerebrum. These central processes are approximately analogous to the strategies for information processing and action with which electronic computers are programmed. With such a conception of intelligence, the assumptions that intelligence is fixed and that its development is predetermined by the genes are no longer tenable.[1]

Not only are the facts and their interpretation which would provide adequate answers to the questions posed above still subject to debate, but it is likely that even if a completely clear-cut body of facts existed, many people would continue to resist the truth or modify it to suit their own needs. Testing is an emotion-laden word partly because it implies the invasion of our privacy. A test is a means whereby we are forced to lay bare our weaknesses as well as our strengths, with the choice of subject matter left to the tester. Imagine a poker game in which all the bluffs are called, and the winner determined purely on the basis of the cards held. A test is a means of calling our bluffs, either in the classroom or the outside world, and since we all bluff occasionally, tests can present a threat to our winning.

One way of avoiding the problems raised by tests is to subject them to serious doubt by saying that we don't know what ability tests measure or that they are unreliable, or perhaps both (which in some cases may be quite true). But we are not flying completely blind. Tests do measure something, and many tests seem to measure the same thing every time. Remembering that we are dealing with a highly charged subject, what can be said on this issue that will help to clear up some of the misconceptions? It may help to consider what we mean when we talk about "abilities."

ABILITY AS A HYPOTHETICAL CONSTRUCT[2]

The concept of ability, like many other concepts in psychology, falls into the category of a hypothetical construct. This means

[1] Hunt, Joseph McV., *Intelligence and Experience.* The Ronald Press Co., New York, 1961, p. 362.

[2] For a discussion of hypothetical constructs, see MacCorquodale, Kenneth, and Meehl, P. E. "On a Distinction Between Hypothetical Constructs and Intervening Variables," *Psychological Review*, vol. 55, March, 1948, pp. 95–107; Ginsberg, Arthur, "Hypothetical Constructs and Intervening Variables," *Psychological Review*, vol. 61, March, 1954, pp. 119–131; and Meissner, W. W., "Intervening Constructs: Dimensions of Controversy," *Psychological Review*, vol. 67, January, 1960, pp. 51–72.

that although we cannot really see an "ability," or locate it in the cell structure of the brain or muscles, we can infer its presence or lack of presence in an individual from his performance. The usefulness of an ability construct stems from the fact that it makes possible the prediction of actual performances in similar, but not exactly identical situations. Thus, it is not necessary to hold a tryout before every baseball game in order to decide who should pitch, catch, or play second base. The pitching, catching, and second-base-playing abilities of the team members usually have been clearly established from past performances (perhaps initially, in the formal tryout, or test situation) and can be used as the criterion for the subsequent assignment of tasks. Of course, the evaluation of an individual's abilities is typically subject to review as the game or season progresses—an acknowledgment that abilities may change. The major league pitcher who has "lost his stuff" and the hitter who is temporarily in a "slump" are good examples of ability change. In all such cases, a statement is being made about a relatively complex and often indefinable characteristic of an individual (for example, major league pitching ability) on the basis of his performance in a test situation or series of such situations.

The more specific the definition of the situation and the consequent performance required, the more clearly defined will be the postulated ability. This can be illustrated by comparing intelligence or intellectual ability with baseball pitching ability. Inferences about an individual's intelligence are made as a result of his performance in a variety of different situations. The resulting definition of intellectual ability is a relatively unspecific one, and information about a person's intelligence is subsequently used to predict his performance over a broad range of actual situations. With respect to most kinds of athletic ability, on the other hand, the performance criteria are specified rather rigidly and the definition of the resulting ability construct bears close resemblance to the test performance, for example, of throwing a baseball with exceptional accuracy and speed. The many factors that may go into even the simplest of abilities is demonstrated by the fact that pitching ability probably also includes such additional elements as the "ability" to withstand pressure and "intelligence" in selecting the correct pitch.

The whole notion of human abilities, whether the ability is throwing a baseball or manipulating ideas, implies a set of responses that are buried deep within the individual. It is obvious that an infant is incapable either of throwing a baseball accurately or solving a set of equations. Yet our usual conception of adult ability, if not manifestly including an inherited component ("he is a born athlete"), at least makes implicit the idea that an ability is something that is developed over a long period of time, is composed of many factors, and resides deep within the person.

Another assumption about the notion of ability implicit in the foregoing discussion is that it is intimately connected to performance which necessarily involves a situation or event. The manifestation of an ability, therefore, requires a situation in which that ability is appropriate. Thus, pitching ability is not required of the President of the United States, except perhaps on certain ceremonial occasions in early spring, and conversely, political sagacity is not required of a world series pitcher. We have noted, however, that the usefulness of an ability construct stems from the fact that it enables us to predict performance in new and different situations. This fits with Baldwin's statement that ability refers to "that characteristic of an individual which permits him to behave adaptively, i.e., to cause the same result even though from time to time the circumstances vary."[1]

WHAT DO ABILITY TESTS MEASURE?

Having acquired some notion of what we are talking about when we speak of ability, we can now return to our starting point, the testing of ability. Viewed in the light of the foregoing argument, it now becomes clear that a test is a performance situation from which some inferences may be made about the hypothetical construct we have called ability. But what ability? The answer is simple. A test measures the ability, holding constant the desire, of the individual to perform the tasks required by the test situation. In and of itself, this answer does not help much, but it permits us to ask two additional questions, the

[1] Baldwin, Alfred L., "The Role of an 'Ability' Construct in a Theory of Behavior" in McClelland, David C., A. L. Baldwin, Urie Bronfenbrenner, and F. L. Strodtbeck, *Talent and Society*, D. Van Nostrand Co., Princeton, N. J., 1958, p. 197.

answers to which may shed light on the entire issue. These are: (1) What elements go into the ability to perform the tasks required by the test? (2) How relevant is the ability to perform well in the test situation to the ability to perform in subsequent, different situations? The first question deals with the variables which influence test performance, and the second with the usefulness of the test score in predicting performance in other situations.

All of this is, of course, obvious when we think of typing tests, tests of stenographic ability, and the like. In these cases, as in the case of the ability to pitch a baseball, the performance criteria are clearly specified, with the result that the test corresponds closely to the requirements of future performance situations. This also means that the prediction of success on the basis of the test score will be quite accurate. On the other hand, where the performance criteria are not so clearly delineated, as, for example in the case of the creative arts or scientific productivity, then the statement that a test measures whatever ability is required to answer the questions becomes a bit more meaningful. Creativity covers a wide range of possible behaviors and it is consequently far more difficult to design a test to measure all of the relevant abilities.

Another way of approaching this problem is to consider a test to be a sample of behavior drawn from a universe of all possible relevant behaviors.[1] In cases where the characteristics of the sample match closely the characteristics of the universe, for example, the typing test or the baseball tryout, the performance on the test will enable us to make accurate inferences about the underlying abilities of the individual and thereby predict accurately his subsequent performance in similar situations. However, in the event that the universe of abilities from which we are sampling is either too large or too complex to permit precise description, we are in the position not only of not knowing whether our sample adequately represents all of the elements of the universe in their correct proportion, but, often, of wondering whether we are even sampling from the right universe. To carry our analogy one step farther, we might therefore find ourselves trying to measure baseball pitching ability by testing (sampling)

[1] See, for example, Goodenough, Florence L., *Mental Testing*, Rinehart and Co., New York, 1949.

the individual's ability to pitch horseshoes. In this case we would probably agree that the sample (pitching horseshoes) is not really representative of the universe of abilities relevant to major league pitching, and we would be reluctant to invest much money in players selected by this test.

It may turn out that many of the standardized tests with which we are concerned in this volume are of this latter type. They are samples from a poorly delineated ability universe and they must be evaluated in this light. Consider the example of a standardized, objective scholastic aptitude test which is composed of separate verbal and mathematical aptitude sections.[1] The assumption on which the use of such a test is based is that abilities involved in answering fairly rapidly, multiple-choice questions dealing with vocabulary, reading comprehension, and simple mathematical reasoning and computation are essentially representative of the abilities necessary for academic success. Since the universe of abilities involved in academic success is only roughly understood, and the delineation of a set of abilities implies agreement on educational goals and methods, the sample of behavior provided by our hypothetical test can at best have only an imperfect relationship to long-range academic success. However, our test does provide, assuming that it is carefully constructed and administered, a fairly accurate measure of the individual's ability to perform the above-mentioned tasks. Such a measure, incidentally, may be a much better predictor of academic performance than horseshoe pitching was of major league baseball prowess, but all this proves is that we are at least sampling in the same behavioral ocean, not necessarily that we have a representative sample.

As one writer has put it, "Tests, then, are samples of behavior, parts that hope to stand for a whole, buckets let down into the great sea of human nature to drag up enough specimens so that the life down there can be recorded systematically."[2] The test-giver is therefore confronted with the dual problems of deciding (1) what factors contributed to the bucketfuls of human behavior

[1] This, incidentally, is the form of the widely used Scholastic Aptitude Test of the College Entrance Examination Board.

[2] Wernick, Robert, *They've Got Your Number*. W. W. Norton and Co., New York, 1956, p. 38.

that he is busy collecting, and (2) what he can learn from an analysis of a particular specimen that will enable him to make accurate statements about the characteristics of the ocean from which it was drawn.

It should be emphasized that these are not insurmountable problems. The analysis has already been carried some distance. For example, we know that standardized tests vary considerably with respect to how closely they approximate the behavioral universe they purport to sample. Standardized achievement tests, for example, because of the theoretically finite nature of the universe (for example, all recorded knowledge in the field of organic chemistry), stand a better chance of meeting the sampling requirements.[1] On the other hand, it should be remembered that although a set of tasks is called a "scholastic aptitude" test, it does not necessarily mean that the test samples all the behavior involved in scholastic achievement any more than our horseshoe pitching test samples all the abilities involved in major league baseball playing ability.

Many of the variables which play a part in test performance (including cultural background, health, personality, motivation, genetic ability, and so on) will also play an important role in other kinds of achievement, both academic and nonacademic. Tests, therefore, may be extremely useful predictors of many kinds of performance. It is, however, of some practical value to have a clear conception of what goes into an individual's test performance for several reasons. First, when evaluating a given test instrument for possible use as a means of predicting performance, it is necessary to be able to analyze in detail what qualities the test is measuring. It would be inappropriate, for example, to expect a test with a high formal learning component (an achievement test) to predict accurately an individual's ability to readjust rapidly to new situations. We need to know, therefore, what we

[1] Because the universe may be relatively well defined and limited, however, if an achievement test fails to hit the mark, it may miss by a considerable margin. As Henry Dyer of Educational Testing Service has put it, "It never seems to occur to some people that the content of a standardized achievement test in any particular subject matter area may be only incidentally related to what a specific course of study in that area may call for." ("On the Reduction of Ignorance About Tests in Guidance," lecture given at the Guidance Institute, Hunter College, New York, July 14, 1959, p. 7.)

FIGURE 3. A PARADIGM FOR THE ANALYSIS OF INFLUENCING VARIABLES

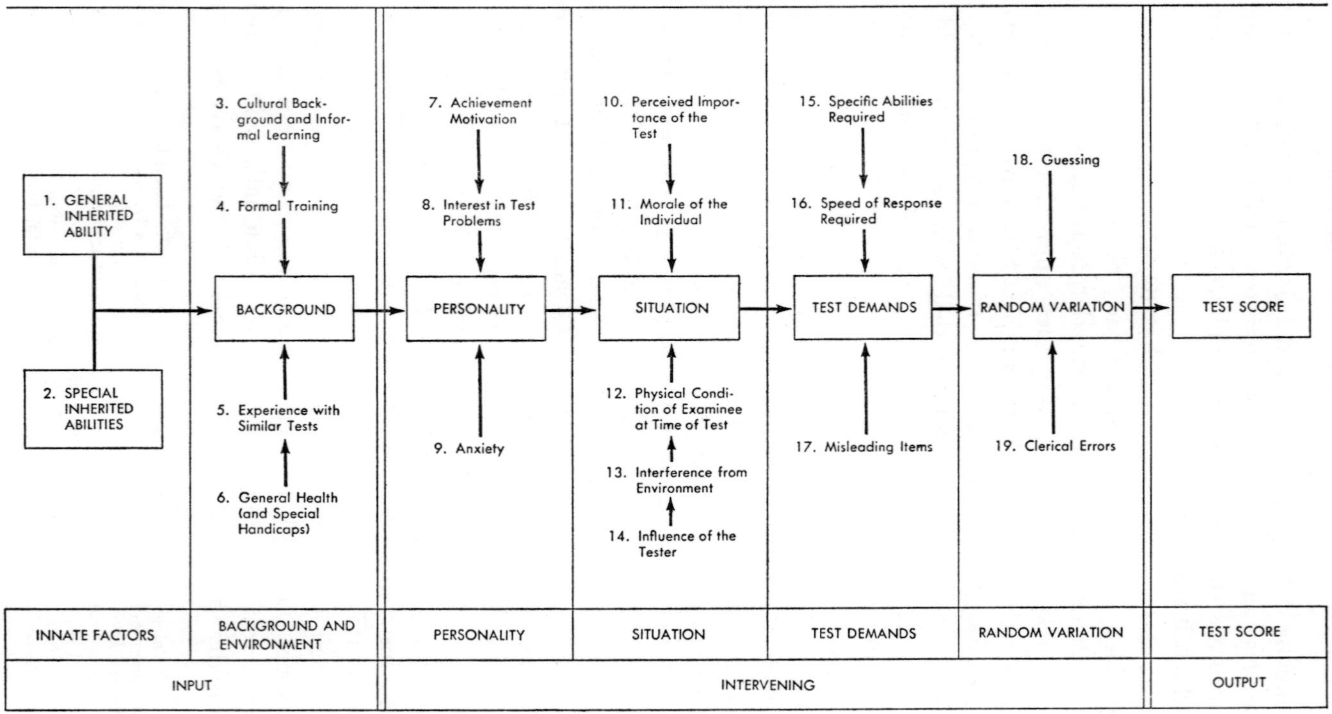

1. GENERAL INHERITED ABILITY
2. SPECIAL INHERITED ABILITIES

3. Cultural Background and Informal Learning
4. Formal Training
BACKGROUND
5. Experience with Similar Tests
6. General Health (and Special Handicaps)

7. Achievement Motivation
8. Interest in Test Problems
PERSONALITY
9. Anxiety

10. Perceived Importance of the Test
11. Morale of the Individual
SITUATION
12. Physical Condition of Examinee at Time of Test
13. Interference from Environment
14. Influence of the Tester

15. Specific Abilities Required
16. Speed of Response Required
TEST DEMANDS
17. Misleading Items

18. Guessing
RANDOM VARIATION
19. Clerical Errors

TEST SCORE

INNATE FACTORS	BACKGROUND AND ENVIRONMENT	PERSONALITY	SITUATION	TEST DEMANDS	RANDOM VARIATION	TEST SCORE
INPUT		INTERVENING				OUTPUT

can expect from a test in the way of predictability. Second, a detailed analysis of the factors involved in test performance may provide some insights into the processes whereby overall test performance and achievement levels of groups or individuals might be raised. Finally, such an analysis may help to explain test scores which are manifestly out of line with other information that we might have about an individual, for example, grades, teacher recommendations, and the like.

A PARADIGM FOR THE ANALYSIS OF INFLUENCING VARIABLES[1]

We have described tests as essentially performance situations from which inferences are made about the abilities required by the test. Two additional questions were raised: (1) What variables influence test performance? (2) Of what use is the test score in predicting future performance, regardless of the adequacy of the sampling? The question of predictability will be considered in the following chapter. In the remainder of this chapter, we will try to provide a paradigm for the analysis of variables in the testing situation.

Figure 3 diagrams the interrelationships between the several factors which enter into test performance. A test score is portrayed as the consequence of a chain of variables, which theoretically might be assigned varying weights in accordance with their own absolute values and the values of certain critical variables such as the test demands. For example, fatigue might have a disproportionately important influence on a test score in cases where the examinee is very tired and the test requires rapid responses. Without introducing a technical discussion of the possible mathematical relationships between these variables, this model is presented to indicate the complexity of the forces which result in a given individual's performance on an ability test, and to serve as a basis for the following discussion of each of the major contributing variables. It should be emphasized that all of the variables will not equally influence any given individual's test score, and it is likely that a few variables, such as family

[1] The following analysis is an elaboration of the model presented by McClelland in his chapter entitled "Issues in the Identification of Talent" in McClelland, David C., and others, *op. cit.*, pp. 1–29.

and school background, will account for most of the variation in test scores in a group of individuals.

Innate Factors

It was the vision of being able to measure inherited differences in intellectual ability between individuals which had much to do with the beginning of the testing movement. Psychometricians are still trying to evaluate the contribution of genetic factors to human abilities. Some, like the English psychologist Cyril Burt, feel that with data gathered from the study of twins, a fairly precise statement about the relative contribution of genetic factors to intelligence test performance can be made. Others feel that we ought to give up the term IQ altogether in favor of a more manifestly environment-influenced concept like "scholastic aptitude." There is, however, little disagreement[1] on the point that genetic factors do contribute significantly to differences in performance between individuals not only on so-called intelligence tests, but on virtually every other kind of ability test. In addition to the many twin studies which point conclusively in the direction of the importance of inherited intellectual capacities, others, including Terman[2] and Hollingworth,[3] have presented evidence from studies of gifted children which support the concept of a genetic component in test performance. The disagreement at present revolves around (1) the size of the contribution of inherited abilities to performance, and (2) whether the most fruitful approach to the question of innate intellectual abilities is in terms of a single-factor theory of intelligence or a multi-factor description of an individual's innate abilities.

1. General Inherited Ability

The question of the relative contribution of inherited capability or potential to adult performance is an important issue. If we conclude that the bulk of the variance in the test scores of a group of individuals is due to genetic factors, then we have set

[1] With the exception of Soviet educators. See Chapter II.

[2] Terman, L. M., and Associates, *Genetic Studies of Genius.* Stanford University Press, Stanford, Calif., 1925.

[3] Hollingworth, Leta S., *Children Above 180 I.Q.* World Book Co., New York, 1942.

limits on our conception of the amount of control an individual has over his achievement, thereby perhaps influencing his motivation to strive for advancement. On the other hand, if we relegate the influence of genetic factors to a minor role in test performance, the latitude left to individual initiative and hard work is proportionately increased. In addition, the former position implies that society might benefit greatly from a determined effort to improve its genetic stock through selective breeding. A greater emphasis on the inherited component in intelligence also leads logically to earlier attempts at measuring intelligence and a resulting acceleration of educational programs designed specifically for genetically "gifted" children. As the British sociologist Michael Young satirically suggested in his fictional account of *The Rise of the Meritocracy*,[1] the "only way simultaneously to get more and better engineers, more and better physicists, more and better civil servants up to the limits set by Nature was to start with the three-year olds, to ensure that from that age on no ability escaped through the net, and, most important, to make certain that the future physicists, psychologists and the rest of the elite continuously had the best teaching they could get."[2]

An opposing viewpoint has been presented by Robert Faris, who writes:

> In sum, we have turned away from the concept of human ability as something fixed in the physiological structure, to that of a flexible and versatile mechanism subject to great improvement. Upper physiological limits of performance may eventually be shown to exist, but it seems certain that these are seldom if ever reached in any person, and in most of the population the levels of performance actually reached have virtually no relation to innate capacities.[3]

A more modest estimate of the genetic component in human performance, therefore, opens up rather startling possibilities as to the levels of achievement to which society as a collectivity might be pushed. In direct contradiction of Burt's statement that "the over-all efficiency of the citizens who make up a nation must in

[1] Young, Michael, *The Rise of the Meritocracy*. Thames and Hudson, London, 1958.

[2] *Ibid.*, p. 48.

[3] Faris, Robert E. L., "Reflections on the Ability Dimension in Human Society," *American Sociological Review*, vol. 26, December, 1961, p. 838.

the last resort depend on what has been called its 'chromosomal pool',"[1] Faris goes on to suggest that "an important part of the relevant causation of abilities is essentially sociological in nature, and that control is most likely to come through penetration of this aspect of the subject."[2]

As in so many debates of this kind, it is likely that each side can lay claim to a part of the truth. There can be little doubt that the twin studies cited by Burt portray correctly the influence of inheritance in the performance variance of his subjects. However, twin studies which indicate that genetic factors typically account for more than three-quarters of the variance in a distribution of test scores have all assumed a relatively uniform environment. The "different" environments in which separated identical twins have been reared are, in fact, probably quite similar. Within any one culture, barring a special educational effort or uniquely impoverished surroundings, it is probable that in terms of the theoretically possible range of stimulus situations, most children fall within a fairly narrow range of environmental influences. Thus, it would appear that Burt's data reflect the magnitude of the genetic contribution where environment is held relatively constant. On the other hand, we have increasing numbers of studies which indicate that we would be making gross errors to conclude that the role of inheritance in human performance is a strictly limiting one. As we become more adept at manipulating the educational environment—physical, psychological, and social—it is conceivable that we will find it within our power to expand our collective heritage of intelligence far beyond our present conception.

Regardless of the ultimate resolution of this issue, psychometricians are in agreement that the influence of inherited ability on an individual's test score depends to some extent on the test itself. A subject matter, or achievement test score, is less influenced by a high or low IQ than is a "scholastic aptitude" test, which has a lower "information component." Henry Dyer has emphasized the fact that a test measures developed abilities and has suggested that "the main difference between the tasks in a

[1] Burt, Cyril, *op. cit.*, p. 14.

[2] Faris, Robert E. L., *op. cit.*, p. 843.

so-called achievement test and those in a so-called aptitude test is, generally speaking, that the tasks in an achievement test are usually learned over a relatively short period of time and those in an aptitude test are learned over a relatively long period of time."[1] However, when we realize that innate intelligence is likely to play an important role in both kinds of learning, we are back in the midst of our previous argument.

A factual conclusion on this problem is not possible at present. We do know that genetic differences between individuals with respect to intelligence and intellectual capacity exist. We do not know how far genetic limitations can be penetrated by manipulation of social factors, individual motivation to achieve, new techniques of instruction, and the like. We do not know whether the correlation between achievement and intelligence is linear or whether, as is hypothesized by McClelland, once an individual possesses a minimum intelligence level the correlation becomes zero. It is likely, as we will suggest below, that our attitudes toward tests and test scores will play an important role in determining their effect on the society, regardless of where the truth lies.

2. *Special Inherited Abilities*

Up to this point we have been primarily concerned with general intellectual ability, or intelligence. The situation, however, does not appear to be quite so simple. Through the application of the statistical techniques of multiple correlation and factor analysis to the performance of individuals on sets of separate test items, psychometricians have come to the conclusion that in addition to (or, perhaps, instead of) being due to a general intelligence factor, the intellectual performance of most individuals is influenced by a variety of interrelated but conceptually distinct abilities.[2] The methodology which has led to these conclusions consists essentially of correlating the performance of individuals on each test item with their performance on every other item, thereby generating clusters of items which are related. If, for example, on a test of general intelligence, the performances

[1] Dyer, Henry, *op. cit.*, p. 3.

[2] Guilford, J. P., *Psychometric Methods*. McGraw-Hill Book Co., New York, 1936.

of the subjects on those items having a mathematical content were found to be intercorrelated (that is, individuals who did well on certain of the items tended to do well on the other mathematical questions, while individuals who missed the original items also failed on the remainder), this finding might lead to the postulation of a mathematical ability that might or might not be correlated with other intellectual abilities, such as skill at handling words (verbal ability), accuracy and speed in clerical checking (clerical ability), and so on.

The list of different abilities which have been "discovered" in this manner includes such factors as problem-solving, reasoning, attention span, perception of spatial relations, symbol substitution ability, a perceptual factor (flexibility of closure, speed of closure, strength of configuration), memory, length estimation, ability to follow directions, word naming (fluency), and "ideational fluency." No doubt considerable overlapping exists between these "abilities," but precisely how much and in what areas is not known. The competing multi-factor conceptions of intelligence range from Thorndike,[1] who suggested that there may be as many specific intelligences as one cares to name (though they might be grouped into abstract, mechanical, and social categories), and Thurstone,[2] who postulated twelve primary mental abilities, to Spearman,[3] who held out for the existence of a general intelligence factor associated with several minor abilities. Further research can be expected either to complicate (by adding new factors) or to clarify (by collapsing categories) the problem, but at present the weight of the evidence favors the differentiation of intelligence into several distinct but related intellectual abilities. It is not likely that we will ever encounter mathematical geniuses who are unable to pass third-grade English. On the other hand, recognition that individuals may excel in one area of mental functioning while being of somewhat lesser ability in other areas, makes possible a con-

[1] Thorndike, E. L., *The Measurement of Intelligence*. Bureau of Publications, Teachers College, Columbia University, New York, 1921.

[2] Thurstone, L. L., *Multiple Factor Analysis:* A Development and Expansion of "The Vectors of Mind." University of Chicago Press, Chicago, 1947.

[3] Spearman, Charles E., *The Abilities of Man:* Their Nature and Measurement. Macmillan Co., New York, 1927.

siderable increase in the efficiency with which we make use of our scarce resources of intellectual talent and at the same time opens up additional opportunities for the individual.

To sum up, inherited mental capabilities probably have a varying influence on an individual's test performance according to (a) the actual level of those capabilities, owing to a possible nonlinear relationship between intelligence and performance; (b) the relative contribution to performance of the environment in which the individual has developed, that is, the age at which the test is given; (c) whether the test requires abilities developed over a long period of time (aptitudes) or over a short period of time (achievements); and (d) the correlation between the specific abilities required by the test and the individual's profile of inherited abilities (mathematical vs. verbal aptitude, and so on).

Background and Environment

The environmental influence on an individual's test score can be broken down into four interrelated variables: cultural background, formal training, experience with similar tests, and the physical condition of the testee. While all of these factors are important, the relative influence of each in any particular situation depends in large part on the specific demands of the test.

3. Cultural Background

There is little question that the cultural background of an individual, including his informal training and the richness of the experiences encountered in the course of his early development, is of crucial importance not only to the individual's test performance, but also to his success in formal learning situations which, in turn, contribute to his test performance. Because tests can measure only developed abilities (in effect, learning), it is inevitable that the child whose environment has been conducive to the development of intellectual abilities will outperform the child whose surroundings have not provided such stimulation. Although much work has gone into the development of a "culture free" test of intelligence, one which presumably would measure directly the genetic component in mental ability, thus far these efforts have been relatively unsuccessful. This has led many critics of testing to charge that standardized tests are unfair to "underprivileged" or "culturally deprived" groups within the society. Several comments can be made on this issue.

The traditional approach to the problem of the influence of culture has been the nonverbal test on which the subject is asked to manipulate objects such as blocks or to visualize the relationships between geometric figures. While probably less subject to informal training than verbal tests, it is obvious that the ability to manipulate blocks is influenced by prior experience with similar blocks, just as the ability to use words is influenced by prior experience with words. The result is that unless someone can succeed in creating a test to be given as the physician removes the newborn infant from his mother's womb, it is unlikely that anything approximating a "culture-free" test will be developed. Even in this case, there is evidence to support the contention that the environment of the womb may contribute materially to the subsequent development of abilities.

Secondly, with regard to underprivileged groups, Dyer has pointed out that it is not the tests which are unfair to the culturally deprived groups, but rather the hard fact of social circumstances.[1] One obvious reason for discrepancies between social groups within our society is that tests like the National Merit Scholarship Qualifying Examination are not designed to select "potentially talented" youngsters, but, instead, to identify individuals who have already developed the abilities required by the test (which, incidentally, seem to correspond fairly closely to those abilities they will need to complete successfully their college education). The tests do the job required of them, that is, they predict academic success with reasonable accuracy. A strong case can be made, therefore, for not blaming the test for the existing inequities, but rather the educational system which makes no allowances for deprived children and the social system which creates the deprivation.

4. *Formal Training*

It is obvious that the adequacy of a child's school environment will play an important role in his test performance, particularly

[1] Dyer, Henry, *op. cit.*

with respect to standardized achievement tests which are designed to measure formal training. To the extent that schools and teachers differ in their instructional capabilities, we can expect to find these differences reflected in the achievement test scores (and to a lesser degree in scholastic aptitude test performance) of pupils having different school backgrounds. That school administrators are painfully aware of this fact is demonstrated by the numerous statements deploring comparisons between test performances of students in different localities and regions.[1] Recently published data from Project Talent,[2] the most extensive study of this kind, indicate that regional differences do exist with respect both to achievement and to aptitude test scores. In addition, Project Talent data verify the existence of social class and rural-urban differences between pupils' test performances, which tend to substantiate the importance of both formal and informal training in test performance, as well as the effect of differential mobility of high ability groups within the society.

5. *Experience with Similar Tests*

A third, and frequently overlooked, background variable in test performance is experience with similar tests. Comprehension of the test and a facility for manipulating the test questions are two of the most important abilities required. Obviously, the child who cannot understand the directions on the test booklet is defeated before he starts. A prerequisite for even a minimum score on a standardized test is, therefore, the ability to comprehend what is required by the test. But, as with any ability, adeptness at taking standardized tests is not an all-or-nothing quality which is automatically acquired by correctly interpreting the directions on the cover of the test booklet. It stands to reason

[1] In a recent report to school superintendents and other administrators under the sponsorship of the American Association of School Administrators, the Council of Chief State School Officers and the National Association of Secondary-School Principals, the Joint Committee on Testing made the recommendation that "all individuals or organizations having access to test scores refrain from publicly using them to compare students, schools, or states." (*Testing, Testing, Testing*, 1962, p. 31.) It is interesting to note that in contrast to this policy, the Educational Records Bureau, which operates a testing service for private secondary schools, encourages comparison between schools as an excellent means of evaluating curriculum and teaching methods.

[2] Flanagan, John C., "Project Talent: Preliminary Findings." Paper read at the annual meeting of the American Educational Research Association, February, 1962.

that the ability to handle standardized tests can be increased through practice, just as the ability to solve crossword puzzles can be improved by practice.

The importance of test-taking experience is recognized by the College Board, which advises high school students to take the Preliminary Scholastic Aptitude Test (PSAT) in their junior year not only to acquire some information about their own abilities and chances of college admission, but also to gain some experience in taking a test similar to the Scholastic Aptitude Test (SAT), which may later play an important part in their admission to college. In addition, high school seniors are permitted to take the SAT more than once. Educational Testing Service, which administers the SAT as part of the College Board testing program, reports that scores generally increase between junior and senior year test administrations—a gain probably attributable to an increase in knowledge and to increased familiarity with the test. The examinee not only gains information about his strengths and weaknesses, he also has an opportunity to learn to think like the people who wrote the test questions.

In addition to measuring the ability to follow directions, comprehend what is being asked, and understand the reasoning of the test-writer, a test also measures the ability to withstand the pressures of the testing situation. Here, too, previous acquaintance with tests may be an important factor in hardening the individual to the rigors of what may be an exceedingly demanding experience (both psychologically and physically). The motivation, health, and psychological stability of the individual are important variables but experience can counterbalance some ignorance and tension.

6. General Health

A final environmental influence on test performance is the general health of the test-taker, as well as the debilitating effects of any special handicaps such as sight impairment. Relatively long-term health problems caused by mononucleosis, thyroid deficiency, rheumatic fever, and the like, in extreme cases, may not only affect immediate test performance by lowering the ability to concentrate and the stamina to sustain high level intellectual effort, but also have a continuing influence on the effectiveness of formal and informal training.

In summary, the environmental background of the test-taker influences his performance through (a) cultural background and informal training extending all the way back to his emergence from the womb (and possibly before); (b) formal training, which, in turn, is dependent upon the cultural background and the skills acquired as a result of informal training; (c) experience with tests of a similar nature, which provides him with a variety of test-taking skills as well as the ability to withstand the pressure of the test situation; and (d) contributing facts of general health and special handicaps.

Personality

Up to this point we have been concerned primarily with the input variables, essentially the ability component in test performance. In the following three sections we will be concerned with the variables which operate to determine what proportion of the individual's capabilities will actually be manifested in the test situation. The aspects of personality which are most clearly related to test performance are motivation, interest in the problems presented on the test, and the subject's susceptibility to anxiety.

The desire to do well on a test is related to actual performance through the subject's level of concentration, general expenditure of mental energy, persistence in attempting to solve difficult problems, and work rate. The relative influence of these factors, in turn, is related to the demands of the test situation. The speed of responses required by the test, the difficulty of the individual test items, and the overall length of the test would all seem to be directly related to the contribution of motivation to an individual's test score. The faster the subject is required to work, the more difficult his tasks, and the longer he is required to sustain his performance level, the more important it is that he be highly motivated to do well on the test. It is likely, therefore, that high level aptitude tests such as the Miller Analogies Test, which is typically used in graduate student selection in psychology, contain a large motivational factor in addition to whatever other abilities they may measure.

An individual's performance may be considered either in the light of his overall achievement motivation[1] or from a "situation-specific" point of view (the desire to do well on a particular test). While the two aspects of motivation are intimately related, the latter aspect is particularly influenced by the individual's perception of the importance of the test and his expectations of success or failure. These variables will be considered subsequently under the general heading of situational factors in test performance.

7. Achievement Motivation

Overall achievement motivation has been shown to be related to social values and child-training practices, and consequently to social class, ethnic, religious, and other subcultural groupings which vary along these dimensions.[2] We are therefore forced to return to the influence of cultural and environmental factors in order to understand the origin of differences in motivation when taking a test. In addition to contributing a large measure to the development of his actual capabilities, it appears that a child's family background may play an important part in determining what proportion of those abilities the child will utilize in a test situation. Evidence indicates that a family environment which emphasized the early assumption of responsibility and the relative independence of children, in addition to stressing the social values of competition and hard work, contributes significantly to achievement motivation.[3] Achievement motivation also has been

[1] See McClelland, David C., John W. Atkinson, Russell A. Clark, and Edward A. Lowell, *The Achievement Motive*, Appleton-Century-Crofts, Inc., New York, 1953. Achievement motivation is conceived as an enduring personality disposition to strive for success in situations whereby the author's performance is to be evaluated in terms of some standard of excellence. The disposition, it is assumed, is learned so that its strength may vary as between individuals. Also, see Rosen, B. C., "The Achievement Syndrome," *American Sociological Review*, vol. 21, April, 1956, pp. 203–211.

[2] See, for example, Winterbottom, Marian R., "The Relation of Need for Achievement to Learning Experiences in Independence and Mastery" in Atkinson, J. W., editor, *Motives in Fantasy, Action and Society*, D. Van Nostrand Co., Princeton, N. J., 1958; Strodtbeck, F. L., "Family Interaction, Values and Achievement" in McClelland, David C., A. L. Baldwin, and others, *op. cit.*, pp. 135–194; and McClelland, David C., editor, *Studies in Motivation*, Appleton-Century-Crofts, Inc., New York, 1955.

[3] Winterbottom, Marian R., *op. cit.*

related to the perceived chances of success,[1] with the result that the child (or adult for that matter) who finds himself in a situation offering little apparent chance for advancement may show correspondingly low levels of motivation. It is likely that these factors have a multiplicative effect on the test performance of culturally disadvantaged groups who may suffer because they lack not only the abilities with which to perform, but also the incentive to make use of whatever resources they possess.

8. *Interest in Test Problems*

Another personality factor which may be influenced by the individual's cultural background is the interest of the individual in the kinds of problems he encounters on the test. The child who for one reason or another has little or no interest in solving problems pertaining to the rates of progress of an automobile, or the price of oranges, is not likely to perform well on a mathematical aptitude test which makes use of this type of item. Interest in the subject matter of a test and the consequent willingness to concentrate on the tasks required is probably related to general and situational motivational factors, as well as to the actual ability of the individual to perform such tasks. It is argued, for example, that a child with high mathematical ability, as a matter of course, will be interested in mathematical problems. On the other hand, critics of tests have often claimed that routine test items may bore the intellectually gifted individual to the extent that his performance actually suffers as compared with the less able but more conscientious subject. While little empirical evidence has been provided in support of this contention, there is a strong possibility, based on the face validity of the argument, that interest in the task *per se* will affect test performance, particularly in the case of younger children.

9. *Anxiety*

The anxiety level of the individual constitutes the third personality variable to be considered here. Since test-taking involves performing under tension (again, depending in part upon the

[1] Atkinson, John W., "Motivational Determinants of Risk-Taking Behavior," *Psychological Review*, vol. 64, November, 1957, pp. 359–372.

perceived importance of the test and the individual's expectations of success or failure),[1] it is reasonable to suppose that for some individuals anxiety may operate to inhibit test performance.[2] In *Anxiety in Elementary School Children* Sarason and others[3] present evidence that anxiety produces inhibiting effects on the test performance of children who are characterized as "anxious." The authors state: "The most consistent finding in our studies is the negative correlation between anxiety and intelligence test scores: the higher the test score on anxiety, the lower the I.Q." They further conclude that this is only partly because a lower ability level serves as a cause of anxiety. According to their data, the bulk of the cases contributing to the negative correlation are within the intellectually average range (90–110) and these children should not have trouble in school. They maintain that "in the case of the intellectually average but anxious child, the estimate of potential based on conventional tests may contain more error than in the case of most other intellectually average children."[4]

The problem of the influence of anxiety on test performance is complicated by the fact that often no one is in a position to identify the child whose anxiety level is high. Sarason has data which indicate that teachers do not typically have the ability or the time to perform such a diagnostic function. As a result, the anxiety level of some children may increase as they continue to perform below capacity on subsequent tests.

In summary, achievement motivation, interest in the problems posed by the test, and the anxiety level of the individual being tested are all likely to contribute to the degree to which he lives up to his potential. In addition, the effect of each of these personality factors will vary with changes in situational variables, which will be discussed in the following section.

[1] See Atkinson, John W., and George H. Litwin, "Achievement Motive and Test Anxiety as Motives to Approach Success and Avoid Failure," *Journal of Abnormal and Social Psychology*, vol. 60, January, 1960, pp. 52–63.

[2] See Grooms, Robert R., and Norman S. Endler, "The Effect of Anxiety on Academic Achievement," *Journal of Educational Psychology*, vol. 51, October, 1960, pp. 299–304. It should also be pointed out that a minimum level of anxiety may be facilitating to test performance.

[3] Sarason, Seymour B., and others, *Anxiety in Elementary School Children.* John Wiley and Sons, New York, 1960.

[4] *Ibid.*, p. 270.

Situational Factors

The perceived importance of the test, the confidence or morale of the individual taking the test, the immediate physical condition of the test-taker, the physical environment in which the test is given, and the facilitating or debilitating effect of the tester make up the situational variables which may influence test performance.

10. Perceived Importance of the Test

Atkinson[1] conceives of the strength of performance in a situation as a consequence of a momentary state, termed "motivation," which is the product of motive strength and of situational variables. In this manner, the relatively enduring characteristics of the personality system (for example, achievement motivation as discussed in the preceding section) are linked with the more variable contingencies arising from the social system in which the individual is embedded, as joint determiners of motivation, and consequently of behavior (or test performance). According to Atkinson's model, two separate situational factors can be distinguished. The first is the perceived importance of the task to be completed (the test) or in other words, its "incentive value." This is defined as the degree of satisfaction or dissatisfaction which the individual attaches to achievement or nonachievement of the goal. Satisfaction or dissatisfaction, in turn, is directly related to both internal and external rewards for high level performance. The perception of possible rewards or punishments consequent to test performance, then, is an important source of "situation-specific" motivation which we have previously noted is related to effort, perseverance, and willingness to tackle difficult problems.

11. Morale of the Individual

In addition to perceived rewards and punishments ("incentive value"), the individual's expectations of success or failure in the task at hand have been determined to be of importance in influencing motivation. The relative frequency of the person's

[1] Atkinson, John W., *op. cit.*, discussed in Crockett, H. J., Jr., "Achievement Motive and Mobility," *American Sociological Review*, vol. 27, April, 1962, p. 193.

past experiences of success or failure in similar situations will provide the chief basis for estimating the likelihood of success in the immediate situation.[1] If the individual perceives the task to be exceptionally difficult (based perhaps on previous experience, hearsay, or a variety of other factors), and consequently considers his own chances of success to be quite small, he may tend to invest less effort. While little systematic evidence is available, from what we know about performance in other situations, it is likely that confidence in one's ability to perform successfully the task required is an important variable in maximizing productivity.

12. *Physical Condition of Examinee*

The examinee's physical condition at the time of the test performance may influence his score, although the evidence indicates that, at least for relatively short tests not requiring extraordinary expenditures of effort, high achievement motivation probably compensates for minor ill health, fatigue, and other temporary ailments. We are beginning to realize that human beings have a tremendous reservoir of "emergency energy" available for situations in which our normal, routine energy levels are not sufficient. In such cases, our supply of adrenalin may make up for at least part of what we might have missed in sleep the night before the test. On the other hand, as the test demands increase, so do the energy requirements and the possibility that sickness or fatigue will hamper performance.

13. *Interference from Environment*

Many have claimed that the physical environment in which the test is given potentially affects performance. Excessive noise, interruptions, insufficient light, temperature, and the like, may inhibit the concentration of those taking the test and thereby affect their scores. There is, however, some systematic evidence here which indicates that it takes a tremendous amount of distraction to produce a significant change in an individual's test

[1] This takes us back to the factor of experience with similar tests which was discussed earlier. It now appears that not only is the experience of having taken similar tests important from the standpoint of practice, but, in addition, the nature of that experience (that is, the individual's perception of his performance) is of potential importance.

performance. Studies in which individuals have been forced to take tests while the experimenter pounded with a hammer inches from their hands support the contention that we have tended to overestimate the effect of distraction variables on test scores.[1] It would seem that interference of a minor sort does not greatly hamper performance, at least for highly motivated individuals.

14. Influence of the Tester

A great deal of data have been gathered concerning the facilitating or debilitating effect of the tester on the individual taking the test.[2] The bulk of the evidence indicates that particularly in the case of an individual test like the Stanford-Binet, the tester can have a significant effect on the test score. It is partly for this reason that the administration of individual intelligence tests usually is restricted to specially trained and qualified specialists. Even among trained psychometricians, however, there is likely to be considerable variation in the rapport established with the examinee and, consequently, in the examinee's performance. This is particularly true in the case of young children.

In conclusion, situational effects on motivation and morale may significantly alter test performance but the physical condition of the examinee and minor distractions are likely to have only a small impact on scores. In the case of an individually administered test, the evidence indicates that the tester can have a significant effect on the test score, either facilitating or debilitating.

Test Demands

A significant factor in each of the areas already considered has been the demands of the test itself. We have pointed out that such factors as the complexity of the test items, the speed at which the

[1] Miller, James G., "The Development of Experimental Stress Sensitive Tests for Predicting Performance in Military Tasks." Personnel Research Branch Adjutant General's Office, Department of the Army, Technical Report No. 1079, October, 1953.

[2] Smith, William F., and F. C. Rockett, "Test Performance as a Function of Anxiety, Instructor and Instructions, *Journal of Educational Research*, vol. 52, 1958, pp. 138–141; Schafer, Roy, *Psychoanalytic Interpretation in Rorschach Testing:* Theory and Application, Grune and Stratton, Inc., New York, 1954, pp. 6–73; Phares, Jerry E., and Julian B. Rotter, "An Effect of the Situation on Psychological Testing," *Journal of Consulting Psychology*, vol. 20, August, 1956, pp. 291–293.

examinee is required to work, and the amount and specific nature of the learning required, all play a major role in a given individual's test performance.

15. Specific Abilities Required

As already noted, the single most important factor in test performance is the degree of correspondence between the individual's abilities (including genetic ability, learning, and so on) and the content of the test items. The abilities demanded by the test may or may not match up with the abilities of the individual taking the test. Just as an accomplished pianist might flunk a typing test, a child whose history training emphasized modern European history might flunk a standardized achievement test that requires extensive knowledge of ancient Chinese history. Or the college student who has developed a special knowledge of the chemical process of photo-synthesis in certain types of plants might do poorly on general achievement tests in chemistry and biology (such as he might encounter on the Graduate Record Examination).

It is often difficult to tell just what kinds of information and abilities a given test is designed to measure without a careful item-by-item analysis of its content (and then, as we have indicated, only a rough notion may be gained). Even where teachers, principals, personnel managers, or guidance counselors are qualified to undertake such an analysis, they may not have the time or the inclination. In such cases, despite the fact that test manuals attempt to provide some indication of the content of achievement and aptitude tests, the catalogue title and description may carry more weight than is warranted in influencing the decision to administer the test.

16. Speed of Response Required

Some tests require the examinee to work under a time limit. Others, called "power" tests, permit the individual taking the test to spend as much time as he wishes answering the questions. The relative efficacy of the opposing methods has been debated extensively, but at least one point can be made with some certainty. The "speed" test, or test which has a time limit, among other things, measures the ability to work quickly, regardless of the specific nature of the task involved. Thus, in addition to testing the ability to solve problems in arithmetic, a test which has a time limit tests the ability to solve the problems quickly as well as correctly. While there is nothing wrong with testing the speed at which individuals work, occasionally it is forgotten that two quite different abilities may be involved: (1) the ability to solve problems correctly, and (2) the ability to work at high speed.[1]

It is at least possible to imagine performance situations in real life when a high premium is placed on the qualities of deliberateness, thoroughness in exploring every alternate possibility before making a commitment, and care in ascertaining that each step in the chain of operations has been correctly completed. It is clear that a speed test might not predict success in such a situation with any appreciable degree of accuracy.

17. *Misleading Items*

A final point concerns the fact that regardless of the amount of care which goes into the construction of a battery of test items, these items are, in the last analysis, conceived and written by human beings. These human beings, either individually or collectively, may have a propensity to think about a problem in a certain way or to see one alternative as the best when in reality another approach might be equally correct and yet produce a different answer. This leads to the possibility that certain items on a test may be misleading or, for some test-takers, unfair. Banesh Hoffman[2] has written on this subject and has publicly displayed a number of test items, taken from well-known tests, which he has challenged test-makers to defend. Psychometricians have responded by pointing out that it is precisely for this reason that so-called objective testing techniques have been used. The use of a multiple-choice format permits the tester to ask as many

[1] See, for example, Mollenkopf, William G., "Time Limits and the Behavior of Test-Takers," *Educational and Psychological Measurement*, vol. 20, Summer, 1960, pp. 223–230; and Wesman, Alexander, "Some Effects of Speed in Test Use," *ibid.*, pp. 267–275.

[2] Hoffman, Banesh, "The Tyranny of Multiple-Choice Tests," *Harper's Magazine*, vol. 222, March, 1961, pp. 37–41; and, by the same author, *The Tyranny of Testing*, Crowell-Collier Publishing Co., New York, 1962.

as several hundred questions in a relatively short period of time. A few misinterpreted questions are not likely, under these circumstances, to affect appreciably the respondent's score. The multiple-choice test thereby becomes, in reality, a great deal fairer than the single question essay-type examination on which, if the student misinterprets the question, he is out of luck.

Henry Chauncey[1] has written that there is no evidence to indicate that currently used tests, such as the College Board examination, are grossly mistreating the geniuses in our society by asking them to answer questions written by and for the average individual. That this might occur is, of course, still a possibility, in view of the fact that most tests are not written by geniuses, but the chances of a genius' remaining undiscovered for long would seem to be extremely remote.

In sum, the small proportion of misleading or misinterpreted questions on present-day standardized ability tests probably contributes to the unexplained variance in a population of test scores but it is not likely, at least in the case of basic tests published by reputable test agencies, that the technically faulty item is a major source of error in test scores.

Random Variation

An individual's test scores vary from one test administration to the next and the maximum correlation which test-makers can get when comparing scores made by the same individuals on equivalent tests given at two points in time is in the neighborhood of .80. In addition to minor changes in many of the factors we have been talking about, for example, the alertness of the examinee, changes in motivation, and situational interference, it is likely that part of the unaccounted for variation in test scores is due to chance.

Random variation in number of right answers may occur either as a result of the individual's guessing a greater than predicted number of answers correctly (even where a correction is made for wrong answers to limit guessing, some variation may occur), or as a result of clerical mistakes made by the examinee,

[1] "Report of the President" in *Annual Report, 1960–1961*, Educational Testing Service, Princeton, N. J., 1961.

such as the incorrect marking of answers on the answer sheet. Each of these factors adds to the general imprecision of the test instrument and makes the test score something less of an absolute. From this standpoint, test score differences of a few points between individuals are probably meaningless.[1]

SUMMARY

A person's test score reflects a number of different factors as we have seen. The major input variables were defined as the individual's inherited potential, both in terms of (1) general intelligence and (2) specific capacities for training (for example, numerical aptitude, musical aptitude, and so on), plus the environment in which the organism has developed. Within the general category of environmental influences, we considered the effects of (3) the individual's cultural background (informal learning), (4) his formal training experiences (school, and the like), (5) his experiences with similar tests, and (6) his general health (including any special health handicaps such as impaired vision, hearing, and so on).

Intervening between the test score and the input variables, we distinguished four major sources of fluctuation in performance: personality, situation, test demands, and random variation. The major personality variables considered in evaluating test performance were (7) achievement motivation, (8) interest of the individual in the problems presented on the test, and (9) anxiety connected with the testing situation. The situational factors discussed were (10) the perceived importance of the test, (11) the confidence of the individual in his ability to handle the test items, (12) the specific physical condition of the examinee at the time of the test administration, (13) interference from the environment during test administration, and (14) the effect of the tester. Evaluated under the general heading of test demands were (15) the influence of the specific kinds of learning or abilities required by the test, (16) the demands of the test with respect to the speed of response required of the examinee, and (17) the role

[1] Educational Testing Service has recently instituted the practice of reporting scores as falling within a probability band. This development makes explicit the concept of variability in test scores and the conformity of this variability to statistical laws.

played by misleading or faultily constructed items. Finally, the random variation produced by (18) guessing and (19) clerical errors was considered.

The preceding variables are, of course, intricately interrelated. In almost every instance, the specific kinds of demands made by the test itself influence the way in which some other variable operates to hinder or facilitate performance. While these are relatively simple notions, it is worth keeping in mind that test performance is typically a two-way process—the test requirements being just as much a variable as the individual's possession of the capabilities which the test is supposed to measure. Add to this relationship the dimension of motivational and situational factors, and the evaluation of an individual's test performance becomes a complex task.

VII

The Value of Tests in Prediction

Of what relevance is the ability to perform well on a standardized test to the ability to perform in subsequent, different situations? We have made note of the fact that tests measure whatever ability is required to answer the questions on the test, and that several variables are involved in this process. Tests, however, regardless of what quality or syndrome of abilities they describe, are used primarily for the purpose of making statements about the future performance of the person taking the test. The ultimate test of a test, therefore, is its usefulness in predicting behavior at some future point in time. We judge the Scholastic Aptitude Test (SAT) on its efficacy in predicting college performance. The Army General Classification Test (AGCT) is evaluated by how adequately it sorts out new recruits and predicts their performance in various Army jobs. The Federal Service Entrance Examination (FSEE) is rated on the basis of how well it predicts the performance of recent college graduates or their equivalent in the federal civil service bureaucracy.

PROBLEMS IN PREDICTION

Assuming that an individual's abilities do not change much over time, a somewhat dubious assumption which will be considered below, a test's predictive value depends on the relationship between the abilities required by the test and the abilities required in the situation in which performance is to be predicted. Thus, in addition to the problem of analyzing the many variables that go into test performance, we have the task of deciding what abilities are most important in an almost infinite number of real life criterion situations. From a theoretical standpoint, therefore, the evaluation of a test instrument often becomes a matter of estimating how closely two poorly defined sets of variables match. Fortunately, test evaluation usually proceeds along a different and somewhat more practical path. Instead of worrying about what abilities go into either the test performance or the subsequent situation performance (except perhaps in deciding what questions to ask), the validity of a test is typically measured statistically by correlating a group's test scores with measures of the subsequent performance of the individuals in the criterion situation. If the test, regardless of what it really measures, predicts performance accurately, then it is considered to have high predictive validity.[1] From this standpoint, if our horseshoe pitching test of major league baseball playing ability turned out to have a high degree of predictive validity, we might be justified in making use of this test on the basis of its practicality alone.

Test-making is simplified, however, when we have some idea of the factors that go into successful performance in the criterion situation as well as some notion of what abilities are being measured by our test instrument. On the basis of content validity alone, tests of scholastic aptitude and achievement are likely to be reasonably good predictors of subsequent academic performance because school success is basically judged in terms of the ability to pass tests which probably require essentially the same qualities and capabilities as are required by the predictor instruments. In a similar manner, it is possible to make a list of the abilities of major importance in flying an airplane and then design a series of tests which purport to measure these qualities.[2] The resulting test is likely to be a good predictor of flying school washouts because the same abilities are being evaluated by the instructors. On the other hand, it is more difficult to delineate the abilities which are necessary and sufficient for success in combat flying, in the business world, or for creative output in science. And most often it is the individual's performance in these more complex situations which we are interested in predicting.

[1] For a careful analysis of predictive validity, content validity, concurrent validity and construct validity, see Anastasi, Anne, *Psychological Testing*, 2d ed., Macmillan Co., New York, 1961.

[2] For a brief outline of the development of pilot classification tests, see Flanagan, John, and others, *Design for a Study of American Youth*, Houghton Mifflin Co., Boston, 1962.

In addition to the problem of not knowing exactly what is required to succeed in many real life situations, changes may take place in the criteria against which performance is evaluated and in the individual's capacity for performance. Even granting the constancy of an individual's innate potential, it should be obvious that with so many additional variables affecting performance, considerable variation may be expected over time. From a sociological standpoint, we would expect extensive modification in personality variables (for example, motivation, confidence in one's abilities) as a result of changes in role demands as the individual moves from one position to the next. A good example would be the shift from student role to professional role, which occurs with the completion of requirements for a graduate or professional degree, or the change in expectations faced by the enlisted man who is accepted for officer training. As his position changes, the individual must modify his behavior in accordance with new situational demands and role expectations. These new expectations, created, for example, as a result of a promotion to managerial responsibility or a shift from training to combat flying, may so radically alter the nature of the performance requirements that the test data become invalid.

That such considerations are not mere speculation is attested by the fact that psychometricians have so far been unable to predict long-range post-academic success, or creative output with greater than chance accuracy except at the extremes of the distribution of abilities.

The problem of prediction is also complicated in the case of personnel testing on the part of government, as well as business and industry, by the fact that most of those being tested are adults. An individual's test score is difficult enough to interpret when the effects of differential degrees of practice at test-taking can be ruled out, but it may be even less reliable when the individual has been out of an academic situation for several years. While still in school (and to a lesser degree, college) and even in the armed services, one is likely to encounter tests frequently. Once out of school and the Army, however, although informal evaluations of performances continue no matter what the occupation, the frequency of formal testing decreases. Such an individual may, therefore, have a difficult time matching his previous performance on similar tests (or the performances of those who have taken tests more recently) not because he is less intelligent, or of lower ability than they, but merely because he is out of practice. Although this is probably a relatively minor factor, particularly in the case of power (as opposed to speeded) tests, in individual cases the age of the examinee and his recent experiences with standardized tests should not be entirely overlooked.

Attempting to predict future performance on the basis of test scores is much like trying to guess the ultimate size and shape of an oak tree by measuring a sapling in pitch darkness with a rubber band as a ruler, and without taking into account the condition of the soil, the amount of rainfall, or the woodsman's axe. The amazing thing is that sometimes we get the right answer.

A Test as a Self-Fulfilling Prophecy[1]

If a child does well on an aptitude or achievement test, he is likely to be given special instruction, attention, or encouragement, with the result that his chances of achieving success are increased over and above what his aptitude might warrant by itself.[2] Similarly, if an individual receives an appointment as a management intern in the federal civilian service as a result of a high score on the FSEE, the likelihood of his advancing rapidly in the civil service is greater because of the test. Thus, getting a high score on a test, by itself, may increase one's chances of achieving success in school or on the job, and thereby adds to the correlation between test scores and achievement. In addition to the visible effects of being placed in special class or getting the best job, a high or low test score may have the less obvious impact of raising or lowering self-esteem, altering the level of aspiration, and thereby changing the individual's achievement motivation.[3]

[1] For a discussion of "self-fulfilling prophecies," see Merton, Robert K., *Social Theory and Social Structure*, The Free Press, Glencoe, Ill., 1957, pp. 421 ff.

[2] Of course, children who do poorly on tests may receive special attention too, and it is under these circumstances that testing becomes of maximum value. To the extent, however, that tests are used in the process of selecting the ablest students or job applicants for the best schools and jobs, this use of the test contributes to the correlation between test performance and success.

[3] See, for example, Thistlethwaite, Donald L., "Effects of Social Recognition Upon the Educational Motivation of Talented Youth," *Journal of Educational Psychology*, vol. 50, June, 1959, pp. 111–116; and Thistlethwaite, Donald L., "The Recognition of Excellence," *College and University*, vol. 36, Spring, 1961.

This, in turn, as we have pointed out above, may affect performance on subsequent tests as well as achievement in general. This characteristic of the impact of a standardized test on the individual is not intended as a criticism of test use or of the reporting of scores to the testee. It should be taken into account, however, in the evaluation of validity data as well as in research on the impact of testing on the individual.

Predictive Validity and Variance in the Distribution of Test Scores

Another point to be considered in evaluating test validity concerns the amount of variance in the distribution of the test scores which are being validated. Validation implies a comparison between the performance of a group of individuals in a criterion situation (for example, college) and their performance on the test. Given the fact that tests are not perfect predictors, there will be a direct relationship between the amount of variation in the actual abilities of the group of individuals and the correlation between test scores and subsequent performance. A wide range of ability decreases the chance of making predictive mistakes for the population as a whole. Let us consider the case of two groups of three individuals each. The first group is composed of an idiot, a genius, and an average student. The second group consists of three individuals whose tested IQ's range from 95 to 105. It is easy to see that prediction of the relative level of academic success in the first instance is considerably less risky than prediction for the latter group, which is characterized by low variation in ability. In the same manner, the Ivy League college which admits only those applicants who scored above the 90th percentile on the College Board examination cannot expect to find that within this select group test scores will be as good predictors of differential college success as they may be in the case of the state university, which is required to admit all high school graduates within the state and thereby gets a wide range of abilities and resulting test scores. Just as it is hard to pick a winner when all the contestants are of equal ability, it is hard to get predictive validity when the range of abilities is narrow.

The Test Versus the Society

The preceding discussion of the problems in the prediction of performance raises an interesting question. There is an implicit assumption in all of the studies which have correlated test performance with achievement of one sort or another that when the correlation is low, the test is at fault. It is perhaps at least worth considering the possibility that the reverse is true—that the situation is "at fault" in allowing the person with a low test score to reach so high a level. Suppose, for example, that the most important jobs in our society are not being filled with those individuals who are most qualified (whatever abilities are involved) to fill them. We cannot really blame our test for failing to predict that the below-average in intelligence son of an industrialist will rise to a position of responsibility as a result of his father's influence. If we were, as Michael Young suggests, to assign all of the positions in the society on the basis of ability test scores, might we not increase the predictive validity of our tests and at the same time improve the quality of the society?

Certainly intellectual ability is not the only relevant criterion for assignment of positions of responsibility in the society. Such qualities (abilities) as social skill, goal-directedness, emotional stability, and moral character are probably just as important as intelligence. But we are probably misleading ourselves if we assume that an individual possessing all of these qualities will automatically rise to a position of responsibility in the society or that all of the top positions will be filled by such individuals. We must conclude that a large part of the error between test scores and actual accomplishments is due to the failure of society to assign positions rationally.

THE PREDICTION OF ACADEMIC ACHIEVEMENT

Over short periods of time, it is possible to predict academic achievement with considerable precision. If test scores and high school marks are combined into a weighted measure, a correlation coefficient in the neighborhood of .70 sometimes can be achieved with college grades.[1] This means, in effect, that if a

[1] If test scores alone are used to predict college grades, about the highest correlation on the average that can be hoped for is .50, which makes possible prediction only about 25 per cent better than chance.

student has a prediction index between 80 and 100, his chances of flunking his freshman year are zero, and the chances of his making a B average or better are 95 in 100. Similarly, an index figure between 0 and 20 means that the student has 65 chances in 100 of failing and virtually no chance of making an honors record. While statistical odds and averages are not very satisfying to the student who manages to do outstanding work in spite of low high school grades and test scores, or vice versa, they are extremely helpful to college and school admissions officers who are faced with an excess of applicants over the number of places in the freshman class. The hard facts of expediency and necessity, therefore, frequently offer little choice as to whether or not to use test scores in the college admissions process. Over longer periods of time, for example from elementary school to high school, the predictive efficiency of the test score-grade average combination is still better than any alternative method of making decisions about future academic achievement.

As has been pointed out, standardized tests are generally a more accurate method of assessing scholastic aptitude than individual teacher ratings which have been demonstrated to be less reliable.[1] As a result, where decisions have to be made about school children in order to group them according to ability or to make maximum use of limited facilities, test scores appear to be the best available way of making these decisions. Testers, however, are the first to admit that tests leave much to be desired as the sole measure of aptitude, and that additional information about the child should be used along with test scores in the evaluative process. It is worth emphasizing that tests may add much to the data which are available to the guidance counselor, principal, or teacher who must decide whether to place a child in an advanced class or other special group. On the other hand, the test's limitations should remain constantly in mind.

THE PREDICTION OF CREATIVITY

Probably because of the presumed logical association of creativity and high intelligence, as well as the continuing need for

[1] See, for example, Binet, Alfred, "*Nouvelles Recherches sur La Mesure du Niveau Intellectuel chez les Enfants D'Ecole*," *L'Année Psychologique*, vol. 17, 1911, pp. 145–201.

highly creative individuals, much effort has been expended in the search for valid predictors of creativity. Most of these efforts have borne little fruit and a number of reasons for these failures have been debated. The most common explanation is that while intelligence and creativity are related, they are essentially composed of separate (though complementary) sets of abilities and that, therefore, none of the aptitude tests in our present repertoire is really designed to measure all of the essential ingredients. The problem, as usual, is deciding just what the important elements in creativity are. The definition of the universe is extraordinarily vague. We can usually tell when someone has been creative (although sometimes we are slow to realize the fact), but isolating what went into the creative effort is a more difficult task.

In a study recently conducted by Guilford and Allen,[1] a list of 28 dimensions of creativity was compiled and rank-ordered by a group of scientists, engineers, and others who are in the business of being creative. A survey of conventional tests of intellectual ability revealed that of these 28 traits, only 6 or 7 were being measured and all but one of these traits fell at the bottom of the rank order of importance for creative performance. Thus, 19 out of 20 characteristics considered by scientists to be most important for creativity in scientific work were not included in traditional IQ tests. As a result of this research, Calvin Taylor suggests that the current search for gifted children may be bypassing more of the creatively gifted children than it is identifying. The problem is that no suitable alternative has as yet been developed to take the place of the "traditional" tests of intelligence and intellectual ability.

The research findings are supported by evidence from several unpublished studies which have been conducted during the past decade by some of the major users of scientific talent, including most recently, the National Aeronautics and Space Agency.[2] These studies all show conclusively that there is no correlation between either the college attended or the student's grade

[1] Cited in Taylor, Calvin, "A Tentative Description of the Creative Individual" in *Human Variability and Learning*, edited by Walter B. Waetjen. National Education Association, Washington, 1961, p. 65.

[2] Payne, Seth, "Good Scholars Not Always Best," *Business Week*, February 24, 1962.

average, and scientific and engineering creativity as manifested on the job. Although these findings need to be examined by the scientific community, they indicate that the "C" student from an average university has as good a statistical chance of becoming a highly productive scientist or engineer as the "A" student from the California Institute of Technology or Massachusetts Institute of Technology. They also suggest that the company which is the first to develop an accurate device for predicting the creativity of science and engineering graduates will be able to bypass at least in part the tremendous competition for top graduates of the highly prestigious schools with no loss and a possible gain in productivity.

There is still another explanation for the failure of standardized tests to predict creative performance. In our paradigm for the analysis of influencing variables, we noted that most of the factors other than inherited characteristics were highly subject to the impact of the situation. For example, motivation to do well on the test was related to the perceived importance of the test. In addition, it is quite likely that creativity includes a larger than average motivational component owing to the fact that we become aware of the existence of the creative individual only when he produces something. Initiative, perseverance, and goal directedness all are built into creativity. From this viewpoint, we can at least entertain the hypothesis that given a minimum level of intelligence and a minimum level of background information, creativity is entirely the product of the right social situational influences. We have evidence, for example, that the degree of anxiety produced by the relationship between innovator and recognizer (for example, boss, teacher) has a significant effect on the originality of the innovator. Dentler and Mackler have demonstrated that the existence of a "warm," secure relationship between the innovator and his social environment leads to a heightened frequency of creative responses.[1] In addition to looking for creative individuals, therefore, we perhaps ought to be searching for ways of creating situations that will turn intelligent

[1] Dentler, Robert A., and Bernard Mackler, "Originality: Some Social and Personal Determinants." Paper presented at the Annual Meeting of the American Sociological Association, Washington, 1962. Mimeographed.

individuals into original scientists, engineers, architects, and artists.[1]

This general point of view is also supported by data collected by Donald W. MacKinnon in a study of highly creative architects.[2] MacKinnon found that "above a minimum level of intelligence which varies from field to field and in some instances may be surprisingly low, being more intelligent does not guarantee a corresponding increase in creativeness."[3] In addition, his data suggest that "if our expectation is that a child of a given intelligence will not respond creatively to a task which confronts him, and especially if we make this expectation known to the child, the probability that he will respond creatively is very much reduced." MacKinnon concludes, that "if a person has the minimum of intelligence required for mastery of a field of knowledge, whether he performs creatively or banally in that field will be crucially determined by nonintellective factors."[4]

THE PREDICTION OF SUCCESS IN LIFE

Although there is a great deal of unsystematic support for the contention that intelligence and long-range achievement are intimately related, none of the studies of gifted children[5] has made possible an unequivocal statement on this issue owing to their failure to control for social class factors. Terman found that not only did gifted children turn out to be successful members of society, measured in terms of occupational prestige, income, and so on, but that they also had fewer emotional problems, a lower divorce rate, and, in general, happier and more productive lives than less intelligent individuals. Unfortunately, however, Terman's findings hold only for comparisons between the gifted group as a whole and other groups of average or below average

[1] Research on this aspect of creativity is being undertaken by Donald C. Pelz at the Institute of Social Research, University of Michigan, under the sponsorship of Carnegie Corporation of New York.

[2] MacKinnon, Donald W., "The Nature and Nurture of Creative Talent," *American Psychologist*, vol. 17, July, 1962, pp. 484–495.

[3] *Ibid.*, p. 488.

[4] *Ibid.*, p. 493.

[5] Terman, L. M., and Associates, *Genetic Studies of Genius*, Stanford University Press, Stanford, Calif., 1925; Terman, L. M., and Melita H. Oden, *The Gifted Group at Mid-Life:* Thirty-five Years of Follow-up, Stanford University Press, 1959; Hollingworth, Leta S., *Children Above 180 IQ*, World Book Co., New York, 1942.

intelligence, and they are confounded by socioeconomic differences between these groups. Within the gifted group, it was found that intelligence correlated only very slightly with success. Other factors such as the social class background of the individual again turned out to be a much more important factor in the differential success of members of this highly select group. The explanation for these findings probably lies both in the relatively narrow range of abilities represented in such groups of exceptional individuals coupled with test error and in the fact that a threshold effect may be operating with respect to the relationship between IQ and achievement. Most high level positions probably require a minimum level of intelligence plus a variety of other qualities which are not measured by tests of intellectual ability. Once the individual has passed the threshold intelligence requirement (which we can assume most of Terman's gifted group succeeded in doing), then other factors such as social skill and family background may become of paramount importance in determining success in maintaining and advancing one's position.[1]

In a study of the qualities felt by teachers and parents to be most important to success in life, Getzels and Jackson found that teachers picked social skill, goal-directedness, and emotional stability as the best predictors of success in life. On the other hand, the same teachers stated that the qualities they wanted most in their students were IQ, good marks, and creativity. The authors conclude that "in effect, if the case may be overstated somewhat, what the teacher appears to be saying is: the children who are gifted are the children I like to teach, but not the ones I feel will be successful as adults."[2] These findings support the hypothesis that academic achievement may not, in fact, be related to occupational success except in gross terms, for example,

[1] See Stark, Stanley, "Research Criteria of Executive Success," *Journal of Business*, University of Chicago, vol. 32, January, 1959. The author points out that "progress in scientific prediction of executive success is severely hampered by inability to solve the criterion problem. Organization rank and global effectiveness ratings have served as success criteria in the few studies to date. Organization rank is questionable on the grounds that nonmerit selection considerations contribute unknown but probably large amounts of irrelevant variance. Global effectiveness ratings are probably too specific to the situations they are drawn from."

[2] Getzels, J. W. and P. W. Jackson, *Creativity and Intelligence*. John Wiley and Sons, New York, 1961.

between college graduates and noncollege graduates. In this event, tests which predict achievement in academic situations would appear to have little relationship to post-academic performance.

THE PREDICTION OF PERFORMANCE IN THE ARMED FORCES

Like all others involved in the measurement of abilities, military testers must wrestle with the problem of increasing the predictive validity of their test instruments. The prediction of performance in most of the critical military occupations (for example, actual combat) is, however, even more difficult than in nonmilitary situations. The same old problems, for example, the lack of congruence between the abilities required in the learning situation and those necessary in the real performance, and the situational variables which influence performance irrespective of the individual's abilities, are accentuated by the unique demands of military life. The influence of motivational variables on performance is harder to evaluate and predict under varying conditions of combat and noncombat performance. In addition, evaluations of performance themselves, the criteria against which the validity of a predictive index is tested, are frequently less reliable in the military.

Although military aptitude testing has been proved to be of considerable importance in predicting training school success and reducing the number of failures, there is little evidence that on-the-job evaluations correlate either with training grades or with test scores. Yet, it is the quality of a man's performance of his duties in combat or otherwise subsequent to training that is the ultimate criterion of the validity of the selection procedures used. This disparity between the prediction of performance in combat or other real situation and performance in the training situation may be explained in several ways. In the first place, the abilities required for exceptional performance in combat may be quite different from those required for outstanding training school performance; combat flying, for example, may be entirely different from school flying. This point has been made before and does not need elaboration here.

A second factor in the inability of military testers to predict with appreciable accuracy the post-training performance of military personnel is the unpredictability of the influence of situational variables on a given individual's behavior. The situation may affect both the opportunities in which an individual has to exhibit commendable behavior (likewise, a quirk of fate may turn a highly able individual into a goat) and his inclination to so behave. It is likely that military personnel are particularly subject to the influence of situational variables because of the authoritarian structure of military organizations, as well as the unpredictability of situations and events encountered by military personnel, particularly in combat.

Finally, it should be pointed out that a large part of the error in prediction from test scores to on-the-job performance may be contributed by the evaluations made of the latter by the individual's supervisors, commanding officers, and associates. Not only do a great many subjective factors enter into any performance evaluation, but, as has been pointed out by Glickman and Kipnis,[1] training school actually serves to decrease the possible correlation between ability and actual performance by reducing the variance in practical ability manifested subsequent to training. The more effective the training, the more homogeneous the performance capacities of the graduating group, and consequently, the more difficult the task of differentially evaluating their performance. Glickman and Kipnis also note that the human engineering specialists have been doing their best to build systems and hardware so as to minimize skill and decision-making demands, maximize the number of people having the capacity to use them, and thus effectively reduce the observable differences between the potentially good and poor workers.

SUMMARY

From the preceding evidence we can perhaps conclude that while standardized testing has come a long way both in technical proficiency and in usefulness, we have, as yet, to use the words of

[1] Glickman, Albert S., and David Kipnis, "Theoretical Considerations in the Development and Use of a Noncognitive Battery," *Proceedings of Tri-Service Conference on Selection Research*, Office of Naval Research, Department of the Navy, Washington, 1960.

Robert Faris, "heard only the opening bars of the overture in the present opera on the nature and destiny of man's genius."[1] Faris goes on to suggest that we have some indications that the production will ultimately be a success, but that we may have to revise some of our notions about what goes into human ability and its manifestation in performance. The shortcomings of standardized intelligence and other ability tests in predicting performance over long periods of time and in other than academic situations intimate that the usefulness of an ability construct, at least when projected onto an increasingly fluid behavioral field, may be limited primarily to distinguishing between the extremes. As society becomes increasingly complex and at the same time increasingly dynamic, the problem of defining the abilities required for performance in each new situation may turn out to be practically insoluble. In a world in which the rules for playing baseball are changed every day, the task of the major league scout would assume monumental proportions.

In those areas where the rules do not change and ability requirements can be defined, standardized testing will continue to be of assistance in providing for the maximum utilization of available human resources. In addition, it is not unlikely that psychometricians will produce tests which, over the long run, will provide performance predictability in new situations by accurately measuring such hard-to-define qualities as flexibility, creativity, and capacity for original thought. Such developments coupled with an increased understanding of the situational determinants in performance may lead to significant advances in overall productivity.

A final alternative may be considered. It is possible that the whole process will be revised and positions in society will be assigned solely on the basis of some objective criterion such as the individual's intelligence test score, thereby automatically giving a perfect correlation between test performance and success. By defining job qualifications in terms of test performance instead of other criteria (for example, "judgment," past record, experience, seniority, or family background), the problem of designing

[1] Faris, Robert E. L., "Reflections on the Ability Dimension in Human Society," *American Sociological Review*, vol. 26, December, 1961, p. 842.

a test which will take into account all of these other criteria would be for practical purposes eliminated. It would no longer be necessary to compare individuals on anything except test performance because test scores would remain as the sole criterion of promotion, job assignment, status, and so on. The present trend in this direction is exemplified by testing practices in government (notably the federal civil service, state merit systems, the armed forces) where subjective factors (political pressure, friendship, and perhaps even "judgment") in decisions to promote, hire, or fire are being eliminated in favor of more objective measures (test scores, seniority). Some of the implications of the logical development of this movement will be examined below, but it is clear that pressures in this direction do exist in certain parts of our society, most notably among those groups which have suffered abuses of alternative means of selection.

It is likely that some compromise will be found, but probably not before many words have been written and much energy expended in the search for new and better ways of predicting performance. Just as the builder of a better mousetrap found himself besieged by aspiring users, the maker of an improved test will probably find a market for his wares for some time. It is worth recalling, however, that the concept of an ability is still a hypothetical construct and that before we go about investing any such concept with the sole responsibility for the allocation of human beings to jobs and statuses within the society, we need to be sure that we have described it in such a way as to maximize its usefulness.

PART THREE

THE NEED FOR RESEARCH ON THE SOCIAL CONSEQUENCES OF TESTING

VIII

The Impact of Testing

It must never be forgotten that a person born to low status in a rigidly stratified society has a far more acceptable self-image than the person who loses out in our free competition of talent. In an older society, the humble member of society can attribute his lowly status to God's will, to the ancient order of things or to a corrupt and tyrannous government. But if a society sorts people out efficiently and fairly according to their gifts, the loser knows that the true reason for his lowly status is that he is not capable of better. That is a bitter pill for any man.[1]

The development and widespread acceptance of standardized ability tests in the United States has produced a situation unique in the history of the world. Never before has any society so conscientiously sought to evaluate scientifically the intellectual abilities of its members and to provide each individual with opportunities consonant with his aptitude. The shift away from the traditional bases for the ascription of status to this new criterion, performance on an objective test of intellectual ability, has occurred so rapidly that up to now, little attention has been paid to the impact of the change on the society and its members. Although extensive research has been done on the problems of increasing the accuracy of standardized tests, few systematic attempts have been made to analyze the potential consequences of the widespread use of ability tests for the individuals whose abilities are being measured, the organizations that are doing the testing, or the society as a whole.

We have little information, for example, about the effects of merit selection (based, presumably, in part on a standardized test score) on an individual's self-image or motivation to achieve.

[1] Gardner, John W., *Excellence*. Harper and Bros., New York, 1961, pp. 71–72.

If, as is suggested by John Gardner, such a procedure has a potentially greater psychological impact than alternative methods of selection because of greater difficulty in rationalizing failure, ability tests may have "side-effects" for some people which should be investigated systematically. Similarly, from the standpoint of the organizations doing the testing, we have thus far failed to investigate systematically the implications of test usage for such problems as the most effective use of manpower, morale, or productive efficiency. With the exception of Michael Young's *The Rise of the Meritocracy* and Gardner's *Excellence*, few works have been addressed to the question of the possible consequences of the testing movement for the society as a whole.

Such questions would seem to be important ones to answer if we are to make the most of our accumulated experience on the measurement of human intellectual abilities. The remainder of this chapter will be devoted to a preliminary analysis of some of the possible social and psychological consequences of testing and to some suggestions for empirical research on these issues.

THE IMPACT OF TESTING: A CONCEPTUALIZATION

The administration of an ability test to an individual or group of individuals can have a variety of consequences. (See Figure 4.) The immediate result is that some information about the individual's abilities is acquired by the person or organization that sponsored the test, sometimes by the examinee himself, and frequently by other interested individuals and groups (for example, the examinee's family, his teacher, boss, commanding officer).[1] This information, mediated by the beliefs of the recipient about the usefulness of tests, and usually in conjunction with other information about the individual's abilities, is likely to have several primary influences on decisions made about and by the examinee, on his self-image, and on the way he is perceived by other individuals. These effects, in turn, may have a cumulative or secondary impact on the sponsoring organization (for example, through its admissions or personnel policies), on the career opportunities

[1] Of course, these individuals may also act as tester.

FIGURE 4. A CONCEPTUAL ANALYSIS OF THE IMPACT OF TESTING

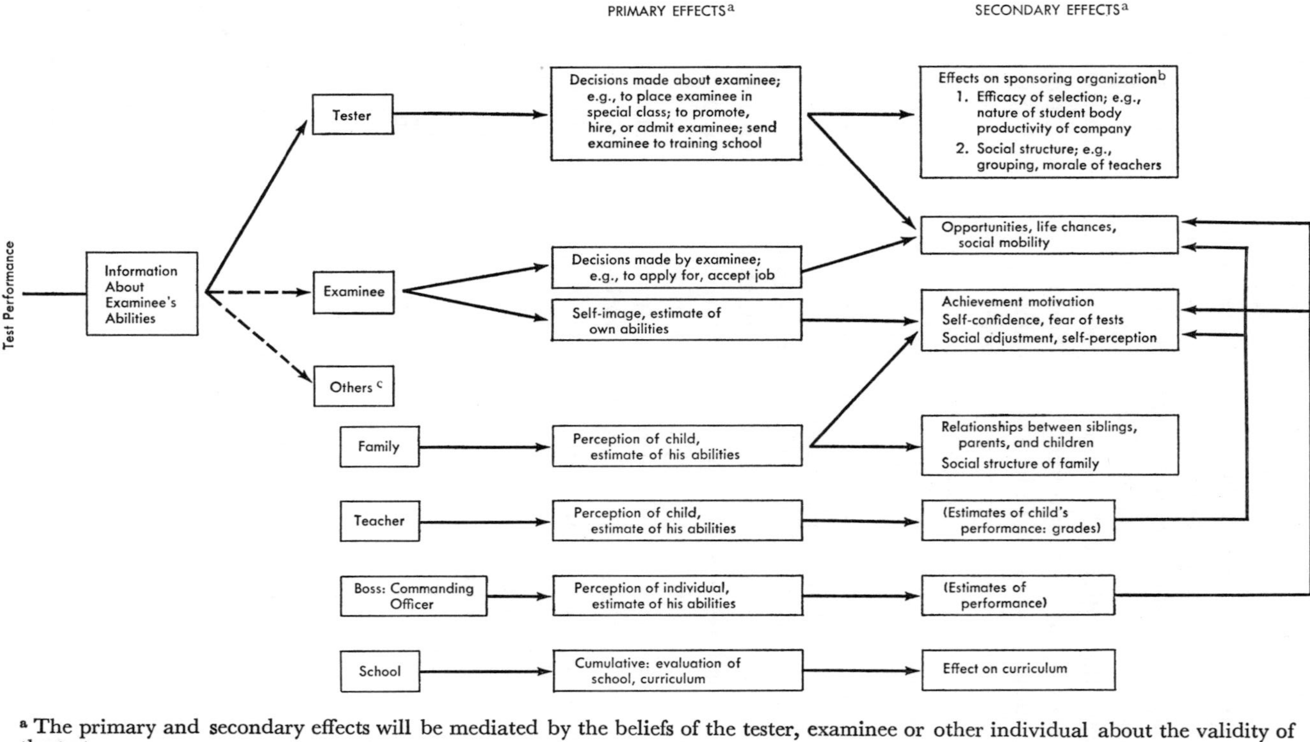

[a] The primary and secondary effects will be mediated by the beliefs of the tester, examinee or other individual about the validity of the test.

[b] The effects on the sponsoring organization will be mediated by the actual validity of the test as well as the beliefs about its validity.

[c] Frequently, of course, one of these individuals or groups sponsors the test.

and overall motivation of the individual, and on peripheral groups such as the examinee's family and school.

It is clear that in all these instances the influences are complex and many variables are involved in addition to the individual's test score. Most of the time a number of factors enter into the decisions made by the organization sponsoring the test; for example, the individual's school or previous employment record. An individual's perception of himself derives over time from continuous interaction with his environment, and is based in part on the judgments of his parents, teachers, employers, friends, and enemies, as well as on objective information such as a test score. Similarly, it would be unrealistic to place too much emphasis on the effect of a test score on a teacher's perception of her pupil or a mother's view of her child. While it is reasonable to expect test results to have an influence on these relationships and perceptions, the score is not the only factor, or in many cases, the most important one. As we have pointed out, all of the primary effects mentioned are mediated by the beliefs of the recipient of the information about its validity and usefulness.

What the test actually measures is important in evaluating the secondary or cumulative impact of a testing program because the effect of the decisions, based in part on test scores, is directly related to the qualities actually being measured by the test. A company might be surprised to discover, for example, that the applicants it hired did not really have the abilities they were presumed to have because of their performance on a test purporting to measure those abilities. The effect on the company, in this case the recruitment of poorly qualified personnel, is, of course, related to the validity of the test that was used. From the standpoint of the society as a whole, the impact of the continued use of standardized tests as a major criterion in the assignment of status also depends on the qualities actually being measured by the test. This latter point will be elaborated in the last section of this chapter.

In the sections that immediately follow we will consider in somewhat greater detail, the potential impact of testing on the organizations using test scores, the individuals being tested, and the peripheral groups and individuals involved.

The Tester

With the exception of testing done solely for guidance purposes, standardized tests are given to provide some information about the examinee's abilities and aptitudes so that the organization or individual sponsoring the test can make the most efficacious selection among candidates for admission, or employment, or in some other situation in which a choice must be made among individuals on the basis of their abilities. The first, and most obvious, effect of a test score, therefore, is its influence on the decisions being made about the individual by the tester.

Although the part played by a test score in a decision to place a child in a special class for instructional purposes, to send an enlisted man to Officer Candidate School, or to admit, hire, or promote an individual is an obvious consequence of testing, *the effect of these decisions*, in turn, on the tester, examinee, and other interested persons is of particular interest.

The potential secondary effects of testing on the sponsoring organization may be separated into two categories: (1) changes in the personnel of the organization resulting from the use of tests for the selection or allocation of personnel, and (2) changes in the social structure of the organization or its method of operation due to increased knowledge about the aptitudes of existing personnel.

A fairly clear example of the first kind of effect is the change that has taken place in the proportion of public high school graduates in the undergraduate bodies of colleges and universities throughout the country and particularly in the highly selective institutions. In 1910 Princeton reported that about 20 per cent of each class came from public high schools[1] and this pattern was reflected among the other colleges in the East. At the present time the breakdown of public school-private school graduates at Princeton, Yale, Harvard, and Dartmouth is about fifty-fifty, with, if anything, more from the public schools. This shift in enrollment has been caused by a number of factors, including the greater availability of scholarship aid, the increasing excellence

[1] Heermance, Edgar L., *The Growth and Development of Selective Admission at Princeton*, p. 26. Quoted in Downey, Matthew T., *Carl Campbell Brigham*, Educational Testing Service, Princeton, N. J., 1961, p. 23.

of public education, and the greater opportunity to apply to these colleges afforded by the College Entrance Examination Board. Where formerly the Dean of Admissions had to rely solely on the candidate's grades, and on his knowledge of the standards of the high school from which the candidate had graduated, the development of the Scholastic Aptitude Test (and subsequently, the Achievement Test series) has made it possible to compare candidates from high schools with lower standards or about which the admissions office had no information. The result has been a considerable increase in the number of College Board applicants from public schools and a concomitant facilitation of the changing pattern of enrollment in American universities. In this case the use of standardized tests in admissions procedures was a factor in changing the composition of the student body (and, consequently, probably many other aspects of student life and activities) of those institutions using the test scores.

In a similar fashion, it may be hypothesized that standardized tests will affect the company or government organization using tests as a criterion for the selection of employees. This effect may be to improve the overall quality of the personnel hired, or, if the tests used are not valid, the result might be a selection of less able employees, with a consequent reduction in the output of the firm or an increase in the turnover of personnel.

The best example of the effect of knowledge about the abilities of existing personnel on the social structure of the sponsoring organization is the fairly recent widespread adoption of the principle that children of varying abilities and aptitudes should receive different kinds of instruction in school. The concept of individualized instruction on a large scale made possible by the development of techniques for accurately measuring aptitudes and abilities has led to a number of innovations in teaching methods and school administration during the past two decades. The most evident of these innovations has been the separation of children into classes on the basis of tested intelligence, reading skill, or some other ability. Although "homogeneous grouping" appears to have been introduced in public schools nearly a century ago,[1]

[1] Purdom says: "Probably the first attempt at homogeneous grouping on the basis of intelligence was made in 1867 by W. T. Harris, at that time Superintendent of Schools at St. Louis, Missouri." (Purdom, Luther T., *The Value of Homogeneous Grouping*, Warwick and York, Inc., Baltimore, 1929, p. 11).

only during the past two or three decades has the practice attained virtually universal acceptance by educators and parents. The majority of public schools today group students according to their abilities, for instructional purposes, in some manner ranging from special classes for the highly gifted or retarded, to uniform classes for all students.[1] In 1954 a Gallup Poll on attitudes toward homogeneous grouping indicated that 61 per cent of the population felt that grouping on the basis of intelligence was a good idea and 71 per cent felt that grouping on the basis of skill in a specific subject area was desirable.[2]

Despite the acceptance of homogeneous grouping, its pros and cons have been widely debated during the past fifty years and a number of studies have been conducted in an effort to evaluate the effect of grouping on variables, such as rates of learning, motivation of students, and a variety of social factors. Unfortunately, because of the methodological difficulties encountered in carrying out this kind of research, the findings on the effects of ability grouping tend to be inconclusive and insignificant.[3] It is possible, however, that irrespective of any educational benefits or lack thereof, the grouping of students according to their abilities may have other effects on the school and on the students involved.

Ability grouping alters the social structure of the school by providing a more clear-cut basis for social differentiation of the student body. Instead of the traditional heterogeneous group in which the less able come in contact with the gifted in many different activities, and vice versa, ability grouping accentuates the existing tendency for individuals to interact more with others similar to themselves. In the process, the gap between children of varying abilities is widened, subcultural differences can be expected to develop, and to the extent that aptitude is associated with social class, a higher degree of class crystallization may be anticipated. This pattern will be facilitated not only by the attitudes of the children toward one another, but also by the chang-

[1] Dailey, John T., "A Survey of the Use of Tests in Public High Schools," August 13, 1962. See Figure 2, p. 64.

[2] Gross, Neal, "Memorandum on Ability Grouping," 1961. Unpublished.

[3] For a good review of the experimental literature on homogeneous grouping, see Ekstrom, Ruth B., *Experimental Studies of Homogeneous Grouping:* A Review of the Literature, Educational Testing Service, Princeton, N. J.; Office of Naval Research, Contract Nonr-2214(00), Project Designation NR 151–174, John W. French, Principal Investigator, April, 1959 (multilith). *See also* Gross, Neal, *op. cit.*

ing perceptions of pupils by the school staff. In addition to its impact on the social structure of the student group, ability grouping may affect the relationship between teachers and administrators as a result of the criteria used for determining which teachers will be assigned to the gifted groups, and vice versa.

Similar secondary effects of testing may be anticipated in the case of business or industrial firms, government agencies, or even the military where these groups rely on test results for personnel selection. Employee morale, channels of communication within the organization, and working relationships between departments or between officers and men are some of the variables that may be affected by the method used to evaluate the abilities and qualifications of the organization's personnel. The basic conflict over promotion on the basis of merit as opposed to seniority is an example of a problem on which the use of tests has a direct bearing.

These are only a few of the theoretically possible consequences of ability testing for the institution involved. Systematic research within context of the organization is necessary before we will be in a position to evaluate clearly the impact of testing on the organization.

The Examinee

The effects of standardized testing on the individual being tested are many-faceted and complex. It is probably the examinee who is most affected by the use of objective tests as a factor in the assignment of status. His admission to college or his promotion in industry may depend upon his performance on an ability test. In addition, his perception of himself may be influenced by his score on the many tests to which he is likely to be exposed during his lifetime. The kind of instruction he gets in school, the opportunities for specialized training, the way he is treated by his peers, teachers, and parents, and in the long run, his chances for success in life may be altered by his performance on objective tests.

There are two kinds of effects which the widespread use of ability tests is likely to have on an individual. The first is the impact of additional information about his own abilities. This information may be the result of a direct report of his score on a test, or it may be acquired indirectly (for example, as a result of notification that he has been admitted to college or from other sources such as a guidance counselor or his parents). Such information about his abilities (depending, of course, on the way the individual perceives the information) may influence decisions he must make (perhaps whether to apply to an Ivy League college or a state university), his self-image or level of aspiration, his attitudes toward his peers as well as his parents and teachers, and other aspects of his everyday behavior.

It might be predicted, for example, that specific information about one's intellectual abilities will lead to more accurate self-perceptions and, in turn, to more adequate social adjustment on the part of the individual possessing this information. Confirmation of such a hypothesis would lend support to arguments in favor of reporting IQ and other test scores to the testee. On the other hand, such a finding might be qualified by the prediction that knowledge of high intellectual abilities on the part of a minority group member in American society could lead to considerable frustration or role conflict based on a failure to move as far socially as the individual's ability might qualify him to move. Achievement motivation probably is related closely to the individual's actual ability level and to his estimate of his ability. Those individuals who are informed that they are of low ability may consequently manifest less achievement motivation than equally low ability individuals who are not aware of their ability level. This argument might be used both by those who favor reporting scores to the examinee (since it might lead to less frustration) and by those who favor withholding information (since it might tend to lower the achievement level of the society as a whole).

The question of whether to tell an individual his score on an IQ or other standardized aptitude test has been a stormy issue since schools began giving such tests on a wide scale. Although there has been much debate on this issue, the trend has generally been in the direction of giving the individual or his family more information about his performance. As far back as 1949, the College Entrance Examination Board took the position that candidates should have an opportunity to find out their scores on the College Board examination. According to the president of the CEEB, Frank Bowles, "This action was taken after strong representations from secondary schools to the effect that realistic and successful guidance required that a student should know the facts which controlled his academic future. Another consideration was that there was no practical way of enforcing the rule that scores should be kept confidential. The rule was tending to break down, particularly in the large schools where competition for admission was keen, advisers overworked, and secret information a challenge to student ingenuity."[1] More recently, the College Board has instituted the practice of reporting Preliminary Scholastic Aptitude Test scores directly to candidates, along with a brief interpretation including the percentile rank of the score.

The increasing tendency for schools to report test results to parents is also supported by Project Talent data, which indicate that very few schools refuse to provide parents with at least an interpretive report of their child's performance. In addition, Figure 5 shows the percentages of schools in each taxonomy group that provide parents with both interpretive reports and actual test scores. Figure 6 indicates the degree of relationship between the percentage of schools reporting scores to parents and the average reading level of the children in the school. It is clear that there is a strong positive relationship here; that is, the higher the reading level the more likely the school is to report test scores to the parents. Exceptions to the general rule, however, are the northeastern rural and small-town schools (A and B), on the one hand, and the big city high-cost housing schools (C) and the northeastern urban low-cost housing schools (D) on the other. All four of these groups have relatively high reading level scores, but the first two groups evidence a strong tendency not to report scores to parents, while schools in the latter pair of categories are likely to report scores to parents.

In New York State a decision rendered by State Supreme Court Justice William Brennan on January 19, 1961, in a suit brought by a Long Island parent to compel school officials to show him his child's records,[2] upheld the right of the parent to

[1] Bowles, Frank H., *Admissions to College:* A Perspective for the 1960's. College Entrance Examination Board, Educational Testing Service, Princeton, N. J., 1960.

[2] *Van Allen* v. *McCleary* 27 Misc 2d 81, 211 NYS 2d 501 (Sup. Ct. Nassau Co. 1961).

FIGURE 5. PER CENT OF HIGH SCHOOLS THAT PROVIDE PARENTS WITH INTERPRETIVE REPORTS AND ACTUAL TEST SCORES, BY TYPE OF HIGH SCHOOL[a]

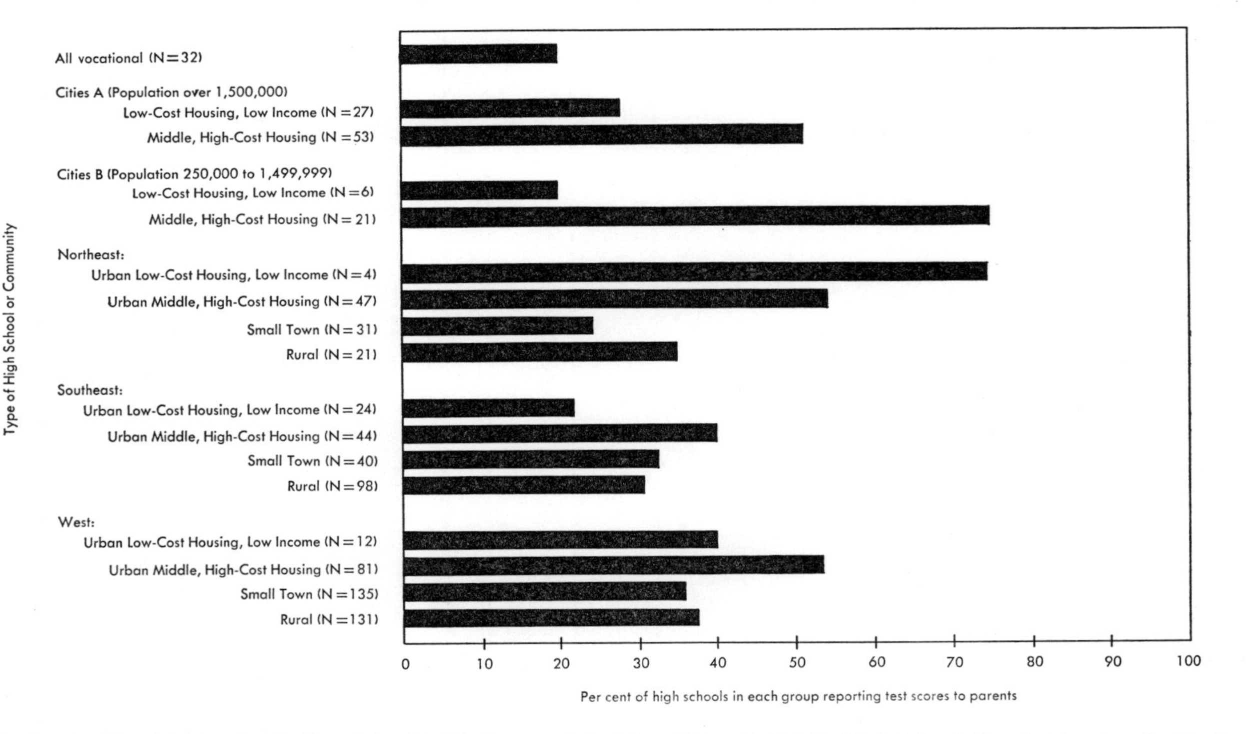

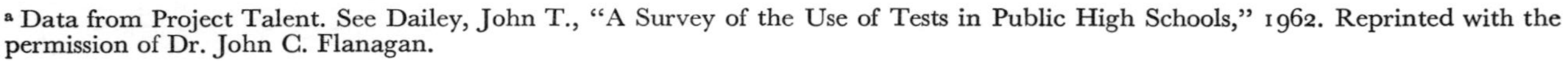

[a] Data from Project Talent. See Dailey, John T., "A Survey of the Use of Tests in Public High Schools," 1962. Reprinted with the permission of Dr. John C. Flanagan.

find out his child's test score, provided it was part of the official school record. The effect of this ruling was to oblige school

FIGURE 6. RELATION BETWEEN READING COMPREHENSION AND REPORTING OF TEST SCORES TO PARENTS, BY TYPE OF HIGH SCHOOL

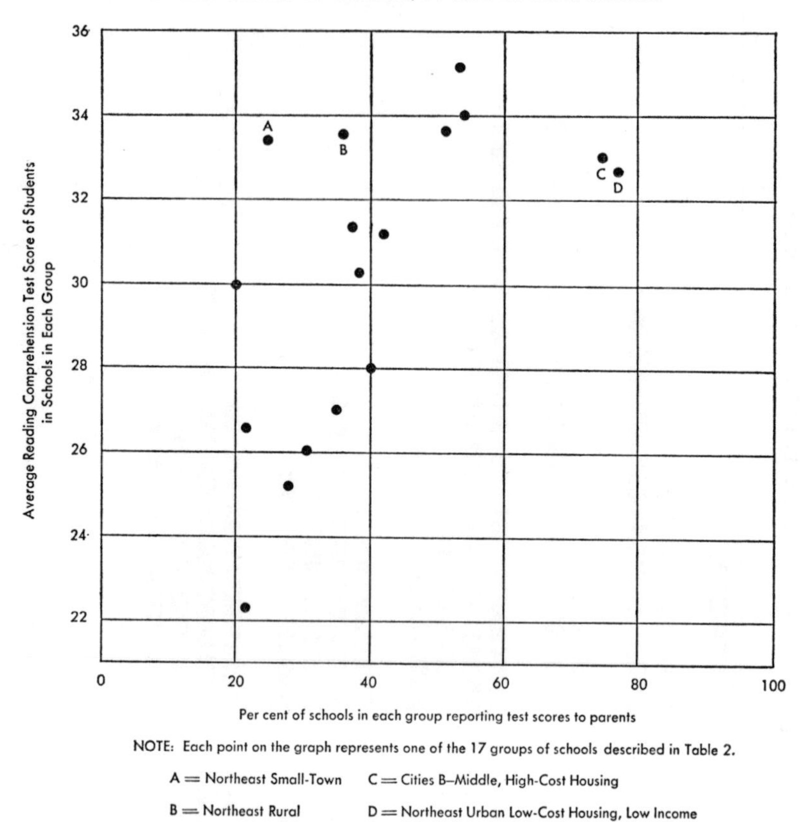

NOTE: Each point on the graph represents one of the 17 groups of schools described in Table 2.

A = Northeast Small-Town   C = Cities B–Middle, High-Cost Housing

B = Northeast Rural   D = Northeast Urban Low-Cost Housing, Low Income

[a] Data from Project Talent. See Dailey, John T., *op. cit.* Reprinted with the permission of Dr. John C. Flanagan.

officials to make available to parents any official records to which all other school personnel have access, with the provision, in most instances, that no information be given parents without appropriate interpretation by the guidance counselor, principal, or other staff expert.[1] While some questions still remain as to what

[1] See "Report of the Advisory Committee on Pupil Records," Submitted to the Honorable James E. Allen, Commissioner of Education, State of New York, August 4, 1961. Unpublished memorandum.

constitutes the official record of the child, there is no doubt that this decision marks another step in the direction of a freer circulation of information about an individual's aptitudes and abilities.

In contrast to the effects of imparting information about one's abilities, some experts note that the withholding of such information in some circumstances can also have important effects on the examinee. In a recent issue of the *American Psychologist*, Lee J. Cronbach, a pioneer in the field of psychometrics, sponsored a letter written by the wife of a tool design engineer who had recently gone through the process of looking for a new job and had found the way paved with a variety of standardized tests, ranging from intelligence and aptitude batteries to elaborate projective tests administered by consultants. None of the companies with which her husband dealt reported the results of the tests to him. His wife pointed out that taking a four-hour battery of psychological tests day after day can become an exhausting ordeal, particularly when no feedback is provided so that the candidate can evaluate his performance. She wrote, "When one continuously must take tests with no constructive evaluation of his efforts other than either a negative reply or no reply at all, it tends to reinforce feelings of failure which, in turn, affect his attitude toward the next test: 'I must have failed the last time, so I'm whipped before I start.'"[1]

Repeated experiences with objective tests may cause an individual to fear or resent the invasion of his privacy that a test may represent, particularly in those cases where the test is perceived as a barrier to the reaching of a goal rather than a means for its attainment. Anxiety, in turn, may influence succeeding test performances, and thus, in effect, reinforce itself. It has been pointed out[2] that as long as there is debate over the validity of objective tests, people will have a means of rationalizing a poor performance. On the other hand, as tests are improved technically, and are accepted as valid indices of an individual's abilities (and are therefore depended upon more in making decisions), anxiety over testing may reach a much higher level. As a result, the reporting of test scores to the individual may have potentially

[1] *American Psychologist*, vol. 15, October, 1960, pp. 665–666.
[2] Gardner, John W., *op. cit.*, p. 69.

greater consequences for his self-esteem, level of aspiration, and frustration level than at present. Gardner feels that we are right to play down individual differences in intellectual capacity because ours is one of the few societies in the world where individual performance determines how far the individual will rise. He points out that we can afford to be coolly objective in our appraisal of such characteristics as athletic ability because we "do not take these as total judgments on the individual or as central to his self-esteem." However, as we move farther toward advancement on the basis of intellectual ability, Gardner suggests that we shall have to exercise greater care in telling people about their capabilities.

The effects of testing on the individual, however, are not restricted to his receiving some information about his abilities. As we have already pointed out, this information is used by the sponsoring organization as a basis for decisions about the examinee, and these actions are likely to be of critical importance to him. In this way tests influence the individual's opportunities for receiving the best education, getting a good job, and, in general, improving his social position. To the extent that a college degree is an important factor in occupational advancement, standardized tests, by playing a role in college admissions, influence the life-chances of most of those who aspire to enter college. This influence can also be seen where a child is placed in an advanced class for special training in school as a result of his IQ test score, or when an individual receives an appointment as a management intern in the federal civilian service on the basis of his examination scores.

In a society that has traditionally maintained that all its members should have equal opportunity for advancement, the impact of ability testing on an individual's life-chances raises several complex questions, both legal and moral, about the use of tests to select individuals on the basis of their aptitude rather than their achievement. It might be argued, for example,[1] that the Supreme Court ruling of May, 1954, in which Chief Justice Warren held that separate educational facilities were inherently unequal,

[1] See Berger, Morroe, "Desegregation, Law and Social Science," *Commentary*, vol. 23, May, 1957, pp. 471–477.

opened the door to a legal complaint about separation on the basis of IQ scores. If it could be demonstrated that being placed in a separate class composed of less able students deprives a child of equal opportunity, then the whole idea of ability grouping on the basis of intelligence might be challenged. This issue is considerably more complex than the racial segregation problem, however. In addition to the question of whether homogeneous grouping creates unequal opportunities, it must also be decided whether the means used to select students for advanced classes is in violation of the constitutional rights of the individual. This may boil down to a decision about the relative influence of inheritance as opposed to environment on an individual's IQ test score, or to a resolution of the question whether people are born unequal.

As people become aware of the uses that are being made of tests, it is possible that the constitutionality of intelligence testing will be questioned, particularly in those cases where test scores are misused. In any event, it is likely that questions such as these will be argued more and more frequently as our educational system moves in the direction of greater specialization and overall excellence.

Peripheral Groups and Individuals

Testing also can be expected to influence other groups and individuals related to the examinee. The most important of these appear to be the examinee's family, his teachers or work supervisors, and the educational or other organization which must assume part of the credit (or the blame) for his test performance.

The Family. The use of ability tests is likely to have a variety of consequences for the members of the examinee's family. Not only does the individual's performance reflect on his family, but the perceptions of the family members of one another, as well as their traditional role relationships, may be altered by information about their abilities. It might be predicted, for example, that information to the effect that one of the children is of extremely high ability (or vice versa) will produce changes in the attitudes of the parents toward that child, where formerly status within the family might have been accorded solely on the basis of sex and birth order. We can only guess at what further effects such a change might have on relationships between siblings, or between parents and the remaining children in the family. As ability level becomes more important for advancement in the society, information about the test performance of family members can be expected to become increasingly emotion-laden for the child and for his parents.

Family goal-setting and aspirations for social mobility may be influenced by information about the abilities of the members. It is clear from previous work on the sources of high motivation to achieve that the child-rearing practices of the family are of considerable importance in producing such motivation. Does information that one's child is of only average ability change socialization practices by the parents away from those that would normally produce high achievement motivation on the part of the child? Answers to such questions must await systematic research.

In addition to consequences for the interpersonal perceptions and relationships of the family members, ability testing also may affect the social structure of the family as an institution in American society. Along with race, sex, religion, and ethnic background, family membership has traditionally played a major role in determining the position in society for which an individual is considered. The structure and stability of the family group, in turn, has rested to a large extent upon the degree to which one's status in society is related to one's family background. As a consequence, the increasingly widespread use of ability tests as an alternative criterion for the assignment of status may produce some changes in the existing pattern of family life in America. The lessening of the need for one's family in achieving status in the society may result, for example, in the further weakening of the already somewhat tenuous ties between children and parents, and the accentuation of separate residence patterns.

Teachers and Other Supervisors. Evaluations of the examinee's work by his teachers or work supervisors will be influenced by their perception of his abilities, which, in turn, may be affected by information they receive about his test performance. A teacher who believes strongly in the validity of intelligence test data may be motivated to "check" the child's IQ score before assigning him a grade in order to make sure that she does not give him too high or too low a grade. In other cases, the individual's test score may have a more subtle, unconscious influence on the teacher, personnel manager, or commanding officer. One study indicated that teachers tend to grade children of high tested ability more strictly than children of lower ability, thereby, in effect, marking on the basis of the correlation between expected performance (determined by a test score) and actual performance.[1]

The reaction of people with whom an individual interacts is perhaps the single most important source of information to the individual about his abilities. As a result, any effect which a test score has on the way the individual is perceived by his teachers, guidance counselor, commanding officer, or boss is likely to influence, in turn, the way the individual perceives himself and his capabilities. Thus, even in cases where a test score is not reported directly to the examinee, his self-image may be affected by his performance as a result of the feedback he receives from those who do find out his score. It might be argued, therefore, that it makes relatively little difference whether a child learns his exact score or not in terms of its ultimate influence on his conception of his abilities.

The influence of so-called "objective" information resulting from a test score relative to other sources of knowledge about the individual is another topic requiring careful research. While the methodological problems in this area appear to be extremely difficult, the importance of acquiring a better understanding of how people come to form judgments of their own and other's capabilities cannot be underestimated.

Educational and Other Organizations. The potential effect of testing on course content and the curriculum of the student's school has been discussed in some detail in Chapter IV. It can be reiterated here, however, that all tests measure not only the individual's innate abilities and potential, but also the adequacy of the instruction he has received from his family, his school, and the other groups to which he belongs. Most tests, therefore,

[1] Baker, Robert L., and Roy P. Doyle, "Teacher Knowledge of Pupil Data and Marking Practices at the Elementary School Level," *Personnel Guidance Journal*, vol. 37, May, 1959, pp. 644–647.

test not only the individual, but also his intellectual environment and those who are responsible for it. As a result of this sharing of the responsibility for a child's test score, his teacher and school (as well as his parents and other related individuals) have a direct interest in the child's performance. This interest may result in efforts on the part of parents, teachers, and school administrators to prepare the pupils for standardized tests, particularly those sponsored by groups external to the school. When a teacher's reputation is at stake, it is quite reasonable to expect her to concentrate on making sure that her students do well on the test. If an entire school is being judged on the basis of the performance of its students on an objective test, it is to be expected that its curriculum and course requirements will reflect the content of the test.

TESTING AND THE SOCIETY

Every society makes use of selected characteristics of human beings in differentiating among its members. In some societies, religion is the principal criterion for the ascription of status. In other groups, one's race or family background may be singled out as being of paramount significance in evaluating one's worth. Regardless of the criteria used, however, no society has ever existed in which all of its members enjoyed equal status. That this should be so is not surprising. In the first place, all human beings are not precisely alike, but manifest a wide range of physical, temperamental, and other differences that invite comparison and competition. In addition, not all of the tasks which must be performed in order for human society to exist are of equal importance or demand comparable abilities. Nor are they equally difficult or hazardous. The rewards which must be given in order to get individuals to fill these positions must be various and unequal. The result is always a society that is stratified on the basis of criteria used to determine which individuals are eligible for unequal shares of these rewards.

The qualities that are highly valued by the members of a society reflect on the nature of the society and the efficacy of the process of status assignment is a critical factor in the society's vitality and possibilities for growth. The Rockefeller Report on Education, of which John Gardner was the principal author, phrased it in these words: "The greatness of a nation may be manifested in many ways—in its purposes, its courage, its moral responsibility, its cultural and scientific eminence, the tenor of its daily life. But ultimately the source of its greatness is in the individuals who constitute the living substance of the nation."[1] If the source of a society's greatness lies in its members, then the means that are used to differentiate one individual from another, to decide which children shall receive special encouragement and consequently to determine which individuals shall have the highest status, will have great influence on the society.

For the first time in the history of the world, a conscientious attempt is being made to measure objectively the intellectual abilities of human beings and to make it possible for those individuals having the greatest abilities to rise to positions of high status. Although many other characteristics of individuals still play an important role in the assignment of status in western society, objective estimates of ability are fast becoming of critical importance as a result of the development of standardized ability tests. To the extent that the ascription of status on the basis of intellectual ability (as measured by standardized tests) is an improvement over other means of differentiating among individuals, the impact of testing on the society may be defined as beneficial. As the skills required for most jobs in modern industrial society become increasingly complex, it becomes correspondingly more important that individuals are given responsibilities according to their abilities and aptitudes. In this respect, the possession of adequate means of measuring the intellectual capacities of individuals is virtually a prerequisite of continued technological advancement.

Ability tests as they are being used presently may, however, have a cumulatively selective effect on the kinds of abilities and aptitudes available in the manpower pool of the society as a whole. With the possible exception of the multi-aptitude batteries currently being used by the armed services, most of the tests that are widely used for predicting academic success or on-the-job performance are fairly similar in format and are designed to

[1] *The Pursuit of Excellence:* Education and the Future of America. Special Studies Project Report V, copyright by Rockefeller Brothers Fund. Published by Doubleday and Co., Garden City, N. Y., 1958, p. 1.

measure general intelligence or, at best, such basic aptitudes as verbal and mathematical ability. In addition, many of those in a position to use test scores in the evaluation of individuals for college admission, personnel selection, and the like have established similar standards of test performance as a basic criterion for consideration. Although thus far, these measures have been proved to be the best predictors available, one possible result of this uniformity in the kinds of tests used and the characteristics most highly valued by those making the decisions is a reduction in the diversity of trained talent available.

Dael Wolfle has pointed out that "in the selection and education of persons of ability, it is advantageous for a society to seek the greatest achievable diversity of talent: diversity within an individual, among the members of an occupational group, and among the individuals who constitute a society."[1] He goes on to suggest that "many of the methods that have been developed for dealing with people in groups have the effect of reducing the variability among the group members," for example, uniform lesson plans, the use of general aptitude measures in the selection of students for higher education, or the basing of personnel policies exclusively on intelligence test scores. Wolfle argues persuasively that maximum diversity of talent with a consequent specialization of function according to the individual's greatest aptitude represents the ideal distribution of abilities and manpower from the standpoint of social value. Although, on the one hand, it is unrealistic and probably undesirable to stress diversity and specialization to the point where communication between individuals becomes difficult, it is likewise dangerous for a society to pass over the idiosyncratic individual who, for example, may not do well on the verbal section of the college board examination, but outperforms everyone in mathematics.

In the preceding chapter we discussed some of the possible effects of testing on individual initiative and achievement motivation. From the standpoint of the society as a whole, the cumulative effect of testing may be a raising or lowering of the level of productivity, depending on whether more people feel that the

[1] Wolfle, Dael L., "Diversity of Talent," *American Psychologist*, vol. 15, August, 1960, p. 539.

increasing use of test scores tends to reduce their chances of advancement and therefore causes a decrease in their motivation to strive for success. One conceivable consequence of a greater reliance on tested ability as a criterion for the assignment of educational or occupational status is a more rigid class structure based on ability. The contribution of inheritance to ability and the extensive use of objective selection tests may accentuate the position of the individual born to parents of low ability. The fact that individuals tend to choose marriage partners from the same social stratum makes it likely that over time it will become more, rather than less, difficult for an individual to improve his social position over that of his parents. We can only speculate about the potential effects of such a situation on the morale of the members of the less advantaged classes and the consequences, in turn, for the productivity of the society.

In the competition between Russia and the United States for world leadership, the differences between the two countries with respect to their attitudes about testing and the measurement of ability may turn out to be of critical importance. Henry Chauncey feels that American testing and guidance techniques may be our "secret weapon" in education, by helping to make our educational system fit the needs of all our youth better than the Russian system meets the needs of Soviet youth.[1] If, on the other hand, we do not pay sufficient attention to the encouragement of diverse abilities and the cumulative social effect of testing turns out to be a reduction in the achievement motivation of the members of the society, we may find that Russia has passed us by.

The preceding comments on the potential effects of testing on the society are, of course, pure speculation. Only time and careful study of the social and psychological impact of information about the intellectual abilities of human beings will resolve the issues raised in the preceding two chapters. It is to the credit of all those who are concerned with the testing business that they have been willing to face the problems created by the use of tests with objectivity and equanimity. It now remains for us to look for ways to resolve these questions without losing either of these attributes.

[1] "Report of the President" in *Annual Report, 1957–1958*, Educational Testing Service, Princeton, N. J.

INDEX

Index